Understanding Your Living Will

What You Need to Know before a Medical Emergency

Ferdinando L. Mirarchi, D.O.

Addicus Books
Omaha, Nebraska

An Addicus Nonfiction Book

ISBN# 1-886039-77-1
Cover design by George Foster
Typography by Linda Dageforde

This book provides information about living wills. Note, however, each state has specific laws about living wills, and such laws can change frequently. These laws are also subject to differing interpretations. For legal and medical advice about living wills, consult an expert. The author of this book is not providing medical or legal advice. This book is not intended to serve as a substitute for an attorney or a physician; it is not the author's intent to give medical advice contrary to that of an attending physician.

Library of Congress Cataloging-in-Publication Data
Mirarchi, Ferdinando, 1970-
    Understanding your living will : what you need to know before a medical emergency /
Ferdinando Mirarchi.
    p. Cm.
    Includes index.
    SBN 1-886039-77-1 (alk. paper)
1. Right to die. I. Title.
R726.2.M57 2006
179.7—dc22   2006018856

Addicus Books, Inc.
P.O. Box 45327
Omaha, Nebraska 68145
www.AddicusBooks.com

Printed in the United States of America
10 9 8 7 6 5 4 3 2 1

Contents

*To the many patients who have appeared in my emergency
room with acute, life-threatening conditions
and to the families of those patients who cried in my arms,
having no idea how to answer the questions
they were being asked or how to face the decisions to come.*

Acknowledgments

Many people supported and inspired me in the creation of this guide to living wills for patients and families. I thank my wife, Silvana, for her endless support, encouragement, and love. I also thank my mother, Ersilia, who was an inspiration for creating this guide. Through her heartbreaking experiences in caring for my dying grandmother and father, I realized the need of many for guidance in similar situations.

I thank my friend and colleague Jerome Wegley for being the first attorney to ever incorporate a code status designation in a living will. I express my gratitude to James B. Caputo, Pharm.D., for his continuous and unrelenting support and encouragement.

I would like to express my appreciation to Rod Colvin and Susan Adams, of Addicus Books; I thank Rod for believing in this book, and I thank Susan for her amazing editorial support. She helped me bring clarity to the very confusing subject of living wills, and the resulting book will hopefully benefit those at risk and in need.

Introduction

This book is not about the right to live or the right to die. It's about the right to be informed, so that you can make the correct decisions with respect to your future medical care options. I have been motivated to write this book by my own professional and personal family experiences and hope that my hard-won knowledge can make others' lives less stressful and complicated as they face their own trauma or that of a loved one.

There are several reasons for creating a living will, and one of the most important of these is peace of mind. An effective living will can help your family avoid the painful process of trying to piece together your wishes. It will provide a resource for your loved ones should they disagree about your course of treatment. A living will should also assure you that medical personnel will understand your wishes for medical care.

As valuable as living wills can be, you also need to be aware of their inherent dangers. Living wills have never been thought to compromise patient care or safety, but their use has not been adequately studied with respect to risks, benefits, or consequences. In this book, I hope to encourage readers to become informed consumers before they draft or revise their living will.

And now for the difficult questions. Are you prepared for a medical emergency? If you already have a living will, do you understand exactly what it states? Might it contain instructions that do not reflect your true wishes? You could face a life-threatening medical emergency at any time. If you become unable to state whether you want specific treatments to save or extend your life, your loved ones might argue about your wishes because you did not make those wishes clear to them. You need a living will for your own protection, to make it easier for health care personnel to understand your wishes, and to help your loved ones make decisions at a difficult time.

The case studies presented in this book are actual patient interactions and outcomes, but they have been altered to maintain patient and hospital confidentiality and maintain compliance with HIPAA regulations. These studies provide a real-world look at living wills and how they are drafted and interpreted.

Read this book carefully and talk with your doctor and attorney to make sure you understand the terms used in your living will and their implications for your health care in an emergency. Use the living will form in this book and make sure it conforms to your state's requirements. In this way you will help ensure it will be correctly interpreted and implemented by health care professionals.

A special note to members of the medical community. My purpose with this book is not to be critical of health care workers about misinterpreting living wills. But rather, I would like to help improve communications about living wills both among medical personnel as well as between medical personnel and patients. I hope you will find this guide useful to your patients and their families.

1

Your Living Will: Understanding the Basics

Do you have a living will? If you don't, you're not alone. Unfortunately, approximately 80 percent of Americans don't have one. Yet, drafting a living will is one of the most important actions you will ever take. It can impact your life as well as the lives of everyone you hold dear. In fact, your decisions, as reflected in your living will, may very well determine whether your life continues after a medical emergency, and if it does, with what quality of life.

Most of us are familiar with living wills as they relate to end-of-life issues. Ideally, in the face of a terminal illness, a living will as a legal document instructs medical personnel to permit us to die naturally, rather than keep us alive indefinitely through artificial means. Having a living will brings us peace of mind—we know we've put forth our wishes for our medical care, and we feel relieved that the responsibility of making difficult treatment decisions will not fall on the shoulders of our loved ones.

Terri Schiavo Case

In recent years, no case has driven home the importance of having a living will more effectively than the news-making experience of Terri Schiavo and her family. In 1990, when Terri was twenty-six years old, she suffered massive brain damage after she experienced spontaneous cardiac arrest at her home. She was later determined to be in a persistent vegetative state (PVS) with little chance of recovery. She had no living will and no durable power of attorney for health care, which meant she had not legally chosen another person to speak on her behalf if she was unable to communicate her own wishes.

Her husband, Michael Schiavo, who was Terri's guardian under Florida law, sought to remove the feeding tubes that sustained her life. Terri's parents opposed the request and sought to become her guardians. The legal battle continued for years, until 2005, when the courts decided in favor of her husband, ruling that the feeding tube should be removed. Terri Schiavo died thirteen days after the tube was removed.

The Schiavo story ignited nationwide debates over end-of-life issues, from the highest reaches of the federal government to family dinner tables. There is one certainty in this story, however. If Terri Schiavo had prepared a living will or had assigned a durable power of attorney for her health care, it would have been clear what her wishes were regarding prolonging her life through the use of a feeding tube. Her family's years of mental anguish and conflict could have been avoided.

Because of the Schiavo case, interest skyrocketed in having a living will and making it available to loved ones and medical personnel. Six weeks after Terri Schiavo's death, the U.S. Living Will Registry, which stores living wills and makes them available to hospitals on a secure Internet site, reported an increase in Web site visitors from 500 a day to 30,000 a day. Still, it's estimated that only about 59 million Americans, or 20 percent of the population, has living wills.

Definition: Living Will

A living will is a legal document in which patients are able to state in advance their desire to receive, or to withhold, life-support procedures when they are permanently unconscious or terminally ill and unable to make informed decisions. This document is a written request that life either be prolonged or not prolonged by artificial means when death becomes inevitable.

Your living will tells health care workers what treatments you want and expect them to perform. It is intended to help avoid any confusion about whether you want every effort made to save your life, or whether you wish to die naturally if there is no chance of recovery.

A living will can also be called an *advance directive for health care*. An advance directive is simply a written statement that expresses a person's wishes in advance. The laws regarding living wills vary from state to state.

Note that your living will has no relationship to your last will and testament. Your living will has nothing to do with your property and will do nothing to distribute your property if you should die. Your living will should not create any relationships between your health care and your property, because conflicts can arise when decisions regarding your health care are combined with the disposition of personal property.

Why Have a Living Will?

A living will helps protect your right as a patient to accept or decline care. For most of us, there is one key reason for having a living will: peace of mind. Having an effective living will means you know that medical personnel will have a clear understanding about the treatment you wish to receive if you are unable to communicate. You can have additional peace of mind knowing that if you should face a life-threatening medical emergency your family will not have to go through the painful process of piecing together what they believe would be your wishes for medical treatment. This document can be especially helpful if loved ones should disagree about your course of treatment.

"I see patients who don't have living wills. In the face of a life-threatening emergency, their families, already feeling traumatized, are forced to make healthcare decisions."
— Dr. Ferdinando Mirarchi

Does Your Living Will Express Your True Wishes?

In a perfect world, your living will would do exactly what you expect it to do if you are unable to make decisions for yourself. For example, if it's clear you cannot recover from an illness, rather than being kept alive on a ventilator for years, your living will may call for doctors to let you die.

In the real world, however, the right course of action for medical personnel may not always be so clear cut, and your living will may not express your true wishes. Let's say you have instructed in your living will that doctors let nature take its course, rather than hook you up to a ventilator for years. However, being on a ventilator only temporarily—for a few days—might be long enough for you to recover and return to your normal life. Consequently, you may not want your living will to prevent such a measure from being taken.

This is one example of why it is crucial that you clearly understand the provisions of your living will. It is possible that the document contains instructions that, if misinterpreted, could result in your being allowed to die when, in fact, you would wish to be saved. The following is an example of the best of intentions on everyone's part gone awry.

Case A

A sixty-five-year-old woman with congestive heart failure was taken to a hospital emergency room when she began having trouble breathing. Her heartbeat was irregular and her lungs had begun to fill with fluid. Shortly after being admitted to the intensive care unit, her heartbeat became dangerously irregular.

The woman had a living will. Like many living wills, it called for no heroic measures to save her life. Her biggest fear was being kept alive "artificially" for years by being hooked to a ventilator. Accordingly, her living will stated that she did not want to be placed on a ventilator. She did not want CPR; nor did she want defibrillation, electrical shock intended to put the heart back into a normal rhythm. She wanted only drug treatment. In medical terms, the drug-only treatment made her a "Chemical Code."

The woman went into cardiac arrest, and her physician ordered defibrillation, but he was told by family members that her living will allowed for treatment with drugs only. As a result, the physician ordered only a single round of medications. The woman died a few minutes later.

This woman did not realize that her life might be saved with only short-term heroic efforts—such as defibrillation. No one had ever explained to her that her decision to use only medications, with no other treatment, might be ineffective. No one had told her that even if initial treatment did require being attached to a ventilator, the ventilator may be needed only for a few days. And finally, no one had explained to her that her living will could name a relative to decide when to disconnect a ventilator if her condition did not improve.

Like so many of us, this woman didn't have a clear understanding of the choices about medical care needed to draft a living will. But this doesn't have to happen to you. You can draft a living will that makes sure your wishes for health care are executed precisely the way you want them.

Support Your Living Will with a Health Care Power of Attorney

Even when you have a living will, it's important to also have a *health care power of attorney*, also referred to as a *medical power of attorney*. This is a document, another type of advance directive, that names the person you choose to make medical decisions if you become mentally or physically incapacitated. The person you choose to represent you is often called a *health care proxy*, or a *health care surrogate decision maker*, or an *attorney-in-fact*. The health care power of attorney is a separate document and is not part of your living will; however, in some states they can be combined.

Understanding the Terms

Health care power of attorney is a legal document. However, you may also hear the term used when referring to a person—for example, "She is my health care power of attorney." Since the term refers to a legal document, it would be technically correct to state, "She holds my health care power of attorney." Still, the term is often used to refer to both a document and to a person. Similarly, there is often confusion over the meaning of the term "health care proxy." Many of us use this term, referring to a person. However, "health care proxy" is also legally defined as a document—the same as the health care power of attorney.

It's also important to understand that a health care power of attorney is different from a *durable power of attorney*. This document names an agent, whom you designate, to make decisions for you regarding your property, finances, and assets if you become unable to make them yourself. Some states, however, allow the durable power of attorney to include a health care directive.

As part of good planning, it is recommended that you have all three documents—a living will, a health care power of attorney, and a durable power of attorney.

The Uniform Rights of the Terminally Ill Act

Passed in 1989 passed by many states, this act allows a person to declare a living will, specifying that he or she does not wish to be kept alive though life support if terminally ill or in a permanent coma. This form of death is known as passive euthanasia, in which death is not inflicted with drugs, but is allowed to occur.

Why Do You Need a Health Care Power of Attorney?

It is virtually impossible for a living will to cover every possible health condition that may arise. Further, your living will becomes active and provides guidelines for how you want to be treated medically only if you are terminally ill and cannot speak for yourself or in a vegetative state. However, what happens if you are not terminally ill, but should become temporarily unconscious or unable to communicate? In such a case, your health care proxy could speak on your behalf. He or she should be able to provide answers about your health care wishes. We tend to associate living wills and health care proxies with end-of-life issues; however, most medical emergencies do not occur only at the end of life. Otherwise healthy people of all ages also have medical emergencies. The health care power of attorney serves as a backup measure, giving health care workers someone to contact in case your living will does not answer their questions.

Here's an example of how a health care proxy can play an important role in your health care. Let's say your living will indicated that you were willing to be connected to a ventilator, but then your condition worsened, and it was going to be necessary to keep you attached to the machine for a long period of time. In such a case, your health care proxy could meet with your physician to discuss whether you would want to be disconnected from the ventilator under these circumstances. Or, take the example of an elderly woman who has dementia and is brought into an emergency room after having a heart attack. She would not be mentally competent enough to tell doctors how aggressively she wished to be treated. In such a case, the health care proxy could convey the woman's wishes to the medical staff.

Because you never know when these questions or unpredictable events will arise, you need a health care proxy to help carry out your wishes. Your health care power of attorney document outlines the responsibilities of the health care proxy, and he or she can work only within the boundaries of your living will; the proxy is not allowed to go against your wishes. Your health care power of attorney will specifically state that your proxy is to act in agreement with your wishes.

Your proxy should also be able to confer with your doctor to put your wishes into effect if your medical condition changes. Your health care proxy also has the authority to refer your case to a medical ethics committee or change doctors if your proxy feels that health care workers are not following your stated wishes. Your attending physician can also call for an ethics consultation if there's a disagreement with your health care proxy. An attending physician is the doctor who has the primary responsibility for your care. In many cases, this is your family physician, but at times it may be an emergency room physician, a critical care physician, or a trauma physician.

Your health care power of attorney document can give your proxy the authority to hire or fire medical personnel on your behalf or allow you to be admitted or discharged from a health care facility. Your health care proxy is not responsible for your medical bills or for any distribution of your property in the event of your death.

Having a health care power of attorney can save your family money and heartache. If you have not named a health care power of attorney, and a health care decision needs to be made on your behalf, your family may have to go to court and ask to have someone appointed as your health care power of attorney or as your legal guardian.

Only a court can officially appoint a legal guardian. Although a health care power of attorney is not a legal guardian, he or she has the same power as a guardian. If you specify that the individual named as your health care power of attorney is your guardian, the court will likely respect your decision.

In the controversial Terri Schiavo case, her husband was her guardian under Florida law; however, her parents asked the court to name them as guardians instead. Ultimately, her parents lost in their efforts to be named guardians.

History of Living Wills

Living wills were first proposed in 1969 by the American lawyer Louis Kutner as a simple device to allow patients to say no to life-sustaining treatment that they did not want, even if they were too ill to communicate.

The health care power of attorney document is not a complicated one; you may find documents online that are effective in your state. Still, be sure to have any such form approved by your attorney.

Choosing a Health Care Proxy

Choosing the right person to be your health care proxy is important because he or she will be responsible for making decisions for you in case you are unable to communicate, even if you may not be terminally ill or permanently unconscious. Many prefer to choose spouses.

Your proxy should be someone who will give top priority to your wishes and act on your behalf. You will want to choose someone who is familiar with your living will and your medical condition, and who is comfortable discussing your living will and your medical treatments with health care workers. It can make your proxy's job easier if he or she agrees with your decisions. A spouse can be a good choice, since he or she will be familiar with your medical conditions and with your health care decisions. Many people choose their adult children, if the children are emotionally able to handle the stress of serving as health care proxy. Choosing a completely neutral person to be your proxy is another way to ensure your peace of mind in case your living will and health care power of attorney should become active.

It is a good idea to name an alternate proxy as well, in case the first person you choose is not available. If you do not choose a health care proxy and a court becomes involved for any reason, the court can appoint a guardian of its choosing for you.

Choosing Someone with No Financial Interests

You may wish to choose as your health care proxy, someone who is not making financial decisions for you, has no financial interest in your physical condition, who has no responsibility for your medical bills, and no role to play in the distribution of your property if you die. A proxy with financial involvement in your medical treatment could create a conflict of interest, even among the most trustworthy individuals. If your health care proxy stands to gain from your prolonged unconsciousness, your death, or any changes in your medical condition, your treatment wishes may not be their top priority for your proxy. This point is driven home by the following example.

Case B

A sixty-eight-year-old male patient, an alcoholic and a life-long smoker, reports often to the emergency room for care. He has a run-down apartment where his son and daughter check on him. The patient was sent to an assisted care facility, but after about a month his family moved him back to his apartment. He was later sent back to the assisted care facility, only to be returned again to his apartment.

At one point, the patient came to the emergency room with his grandson, who told the staff that the man's son and daughter were dividing the patient's Social Security check. They received the check only if the patient was at home; if the patient was in the assisted care facility, the facility received the check. The son and daughter had been taking the patient back to his apartment so that they could continue getting his check.

If the patient had identified a health care proxy with no financial interest in his medical condition to act as his guardian, his health would have been the primary concern.

Although the son and daughter in this example had financial gain in mind, it's possible that your proxy might feel guilty for carrying out your health care wishes if he or she would gain financially from doing so. Choosing someone as your proxy with no financial interest avoids such potential conflicts.

Working with Your Health Care Proxy

Once you have chosen a health care proxy, you need to discuss the responsibilities you want him or her to assume. Make sure that the person is willing and emotionally capable of acting as your proxy. You will also want to ensure that your proxy understands everything you have in your living will. Because your proxy will address questions that are not covered by the living will, he or she will also need to know any intentions and any information the living will does not specifically address. The individual acting as your proxy should understand any limitations placed on him or her. For example, if your religious beliefs preclude specific types of treatment, such as blood transfusions, sterilization, or amputation, he or she should realize the legal document would identify these limitations. You both should also be aware of any limitations placed on your proxy by state laws. In some states, a proxy's power to consent to or refuse certain kinds of treatment is limited.

Your proxy should also know that in most states health care providers are not required to follow the directives of the proxy if those orders are in conflict with what the health care provider thinks best. But most states also require that an opposing physician transfer the patient to a provider who is willing to follow the requests of the proxy.

If your health care proxy has no responsibility for your medical bills and has no role to play in the distribution of your property if you die, it avoids the possibility of conflict. Some people prefer to choose someone with no financial interests.

Finally, it's important that both you and your health care proxy be aware of how living wills may be misinterpreted. Relying solely on medical professionals does not sufficiently guarantee your wishes will be followed during an emergency. Make sure you and your health care proxy understand the potential hidden dangers in your living will. It's your life, and it's important that you avoid pitfalls and make sure your living will does what you want it to do.

Terms to Remember

Advance Directive: A legal statement signed by you, as a living, competent person, that expresses your wishes in advance of an emergency that makes you otherwise unable to convey your decisions. A living will is a type of advance directive.

Living Will: A written document detailing the health care you want to receive if you are in a terminal condition and cannot speak for yourself or if you are in a persistent vegetative state.

Durable Power of Attorney for Health Care: A document allowing another or others to make health care decisions when you are not able to. Authorized by state law, this document allows you to designate another person to have powers, which you specify in the document. These powers can be limited to health care decisions, or may include general financial management, health and medical care, and emergencies. As the principal, you can revoke this document at any time if you remain competent. Also known as medical power of attorney.

Health Care Proxy: The person you designate to make health care decisions for you if you are rendered incapable of making your wishes known. In some circles, a health care proxy also is referred to as being a health care power of attorney document.

Durable Power of Attorney: A legal document that assigns legal authority to another person so he or she can make property, financial, and other legal decisions for you if you are unable to do so for yourself. In some states, health care decisions can be added to the responsibilities of the durable power of attorney.

Last Will and Testament: A legal document that states your intentions and what you wish to be done regarding disposal of your property after your death. Your last will and testament is not related to your living will.

2

The Hidden Dangers
in Living Wills

E
ven though living wills are developed to alleviate pain and suffering for patients and families, they have inherent dangers. The greatest of these dangers is the possible misinterpretation of the patient's true wishes by medical personnel. Living wills often contain such terms as "terminal condition," "incurable illness," or "seriously incapacitating," leaving the interpretation of such terms to physicians. One physician may view a patient as needing aggressive treatment while another physician might say that treatment should be withdrawn.

Understanding the potential problems in your living will and the damage they could cause can mean the difference between your wishes being followed and long, destructive conflicts among family members about how you intended for your medical care to be carried out. Simply put, avoiding these problems can mean the difference between life and death.

Potential problems in living wills include:

- Living wills may be misinterpreted as "Do Not Resuscitate" (DNR) orders or "Do Not Treat" orders. Further, living wills lack code status designations that medical personnel would readily understand.

- Living wills are often not individualized for the patient and his/her medical condition.
- Living wills often lack informed consent—a patient may not fully understand the document he/she has signed.

It's crucial that you understand these matters before you begin preparing or revising your living will. These problems can make living wills useless or, worse, cause them to be misunderstood by health care workers so that patients are subject to treatments they do not want or are not treated when they wish to be.

Problem: Misinterpretation of Code Status Designation

"What is the patient's code status?" is a question asked thousands of times every day by health care workers as patients are admitted to hospitals, emergency rooms, and nursing homes across the country. A code status designation tells health care personnel how far they should go to save a patient's life. For example, a "Full Code" means that medical personnel will use every means available to save the life of the patient. At the other end of the treatment spectrum is the code status, "DNR," which stands for "Do Not Resuscitate." As the name implies, this code means do not attempt to restart a heart or breathing once they have stopped. Typically, this code is applied to those patients who are nearing death and have expressed through a living will that they do not wish to be kept alive by heroic means.

Herein lies the problem. There is a risk of health care workers automatically interpreting a living will as a DNR order or a "Do Not Treat" order. However, a DNR order is never intended to tell health care personnel to abandon all treatment. A patient's code status should be considered as DNR *only* if he or she has no heartbeat or is not breathing. In other situations, most of us would want to have our lives saved if possible. But once our living wills are interpreted as meaning we wish to be treated as a DNR, there is a likelihood that initial lifesaving measures will not be taken.

"I'm not criticizing the medical profession about misinterpretations of living wills. I'm trying to create greater clarity that will help patients and the doctors who treat them."
—Dr. Ferdinando Mirarchi

How Real Is the Risk of Misinterpretation?

Living wills have not been adequately studied with respect to risks, benefits, and consequences. Most of us don't think living wills could compromise patient care or safety; however, serious problems have been associated with the misinterpretation of living wills. In this age of modern medicine and high-tech equipment, it is likely that medical personnel would misinterpret a living will? The answer is yes, according to one research study.

In the study,* four hundred health care personnel—doctors, nurses, paramedics, and emergency medical technicians—were asked to review a hypothetical living will and assign a code status designation. The majority, 79 percent of the medical personnel, decided the patient should be treated as DNR. However, 21 percent chose the designation of Full Code, meaning the patient

---

*   Mirarchi, Ferdinando, D.O., et al. *Initial Patient Safety Investigations and the Living Will.* 2006.

should be treated aggressively. The correct designation should have been Full Code.

The consequences of differing opinions and the ensuing confusion can affect patient safety, as the following cases demonstrate. In Case C, a patient admitted to the hospital with heart trouble had two physicians with very different interpretations of how his condition should be handled, given his living will.

Case C

Mr. A is an eighty-two-year-old male with a history of cardiac disease; he has an *automated implanted cardiac defibrillator* (AICD) to prevent sudden cardiac arrest. Despite his medical history, Mr. A still enjoys a very active retirement and good quality of life. Mr. A came to an emergency department with a chief complaint of chest pain.

The emergency department (ED) physician reviewed his history, EKG, chest X-ray, and lab work. The ED physician felt the patient was suffering from unstable angina, a condition similar to a heart attack, which requires aggressive treatment. The emergency physician treated him accordingly, then contacted the patient's *primary care physician* (PCP) about admitting the man. The PCP then advised the emergency physician that the patient did not need to be admitted since he had a living will and his code status was a DNR (Do Not Resuscitate).

The ED physician reviewed the living will and insisted that the patient be admitted to the hospital for treatment. The patient was admitted and underwent an evaluation of his chest pain and was discharged within twenty-four hours. His treatment as an inpatient consisted of blood work and a chest .

X-ray. Mr. A was then to have an outpatient appointment in ten days.

Mr. A returned to the emergency department three days later with an acute myocardial infarction, or heart attack. The ED physician at that time treated him accordingly and notified the cardiologist of the patient's condition. The patient was taken for an angioplasty; he also had a stent implanted to keep a blood vessel open. His hospital course thereafter was uncomplicated and he was discharged from the hospital.

Including Code Status in Your Living Will

Living wills typically do not contain code status designations. If they did, the code status designation would remove any doubt for medical personnel and family about what level of health care you wish to receive. By having a clear understanding of these code status designations and incorporating them into your living will, you can significantly decrease the risk of health care workers misinterpreting your living will and delaying or withholding medical treatments that could save your life. If this information is not listed in your living will, health care personnel will assess the situation, confer with your next of kin, and proceed with treatment accordingly. The treatment may, or may not, be in line with your true intentions.

As you can see from the next case study, determining the patient's code status is vitally important.

Case D

Mrs. B is a sixty-year-year-old female with a past history of hypertension. She recently retired and enjoys a very active life style. She suffered a fall as the result of slipping on ice, injuring her right lower extremity. She required admission to the hospital for surgery. At the time of her admission, she was asked if she had a living will. She responded in the affirmative and provided a copy. Mrs. B then underwent surgery on her lower right leg.

On the second day after her surgery, Mrs. B developed upper gastrointestinal bleeding. The nurse at the time looked at her chart, saw her living will, and felt the code status of the patient was a DNR. One hour and forty minutes later, the nurse attempted to call the orthopedic surgeon who had admitted the patient to the hospital and performed the surgery. The on-call physician returned the call. The nurse advised him of the patient's condition and of her DNR code status. The physician asked if the patient needed to be transferred to the intensive care unit. The nurse said the patient was a DNR and she was not transferred.

A routine consult was placed to the medicine and surgical service. Those evaluations, fortunately, were completed one hour later. The primary care physician and the surgeon then acted quickly and transferred her to the intensive care unit; she underwent emergency surgery. She was discharged to her home one week later.

As you can see from the example of Mrs. B., it is vital that you speak with your physician to be correctly educated about code status and choose the appropriate code status for your living will. Doing so promotes your safety and protects your right to choose.

The following code status designations are those listed in the Medical Living Will with Code Status appearing in Appendix A.

Full Code

A Full Code is the most extensive course of treatment. Such a code designation in a living will instructs health care workers to do everything in their power to keep you alive. Their efforts would include resuscitation to restore your heartbeat if it should stop. Such treatment should be continued unless your condition stopped improving and you became unable to make your own decisions. At this time, health care workers would turn to your specific treatment wishes, also recorded in your living will. Depending upon individual state laws, the living will may require two doctors—your doctor and a specialist—to make the decision that your condition has stopped improving.

The Full Code is typically the right code status designation for young people and those who are in generally good health to include in their living wills. If you enter the hospital with no living will, your code status is presumed to be Full Code, and you will receive all life-saving treatments available.

Recommended Code:
Full Code Except Cardiac Arrest

You won't hear this code being used in hospitals. It's not part of the common vocabulary among health care professionals. However, if you adopt this code status into your living will, you would be making your wishes very clear to physicians. This code status is similar the Full Code with one important exception—if you were to go into cardiac arrest, you would not receive treatment to be revived. This code status is, in effect, a safer designation than the DNR code; you would still receive aggressive treatment up until the time your heart stops and you lapse into permanent unconsciousness.

Keep in mind that even if you are treated aggressively, your family, or health care proxy can always have the treatment withdrawn later if it is determined that your condition will not improve.

Note that, even though this code calls for no resuscitation if cardiac arrest occurs, there would be situations in which a physician would attempt to restore your heartbeat, depending on your health condition at the time. For example, a patient who has had a heart attack may go into cardiac arrest, but may respond to defibrillation, in which an electric shock restores the heartbeat.

What is the likelihood of a patient remaining in a coma after being resuscitated? Most patients who are resuscitated after cardiac arrest survive provided they begin breathing and wake up. However, those who do not awaken within several days after having their hearts restarted, usually die within several days. In some cases, of course, they die because life support was withdrawn.

Comfort Care/Hospice Care

If you choose Comfort Care or Hospice Care for your living will code status, you would essentially be asking health care workers to make you comfortable and relieve any pain or anxiety you may be feeling, but not to take measures to save or extend your life. Hospice Care means that you leave the hospital entirely, and in most cases, return home. You can also choose not to go to the emergency room at all and have Hospice Care workers come to your home. When you enter Hospice Care, hospice workers will make every effort to see that you are comfortable and free of pain and anxiety as you prepare for death.

Some hospitals and health care facilities have a Comfort Code that allows patients to choose not to receive lifesaving treatments. Similarly, many nursing homes and assisted care facilities offer a Do Not Transfer order to residents so that they can choose not to go to the emergency room if a life-threatening emergency arises. Without those orders, residents can find themselves being taken to the emergency room even if they prefer to remain with loved ones as they near death.

Choosing Comfort Care or Hospice Care on your living will allows you to focus on the end of your life in the company of friends and family, without pain or fear, and with the constant support of Hospice Care workers.

Also included under this code status is the right, if you are mentally competent, to refuse any treatment at all. If you do so, you do not necessarily have to go into hospice care. The explanatory notes you provide in your living will should make your wishes clear to loved ones and health care providers that you do not, no matter what the apparent circumstances, want to be confined to a hospital and undergo treatment of any nature. This clarity increases the chances your wishes will be honored and it releases the hospital and staff from liability.

Your living will should offer a series of statements clarifying your decisions and telling health care workers specifically that you do or do not want them to perform emergency treatments or treatments that would extend your life. It also gives permission for health care workers to stop giving you such treatments if they have already begun. These provisions will allow health care workers to stop treating you if they presumed your code status was Full Code before seeing your living will.

Why "DNR" Should not Be in Your Living Will

You've already read that the Do Not Resuscitate (DNR) code status can result in confusion for health care professionals as well as for family and friends. In the worst-case scenario, a patient can be allowed to die when with proper treatment the patient would have recovered. To be safe, make sure that your living will does not contain the code status DNR. As explained, the Full Code Except Cardiac Arrest will serve you better.

Also note that some hospitals have policies stating that DNR patients are not to be admitted to their intensive care units. More than likely, you would not be told of this policy, and the patient is sent to a floor with a lower level of care. In order to be treated, you would need to be moved to a hospital that has no such policy. Ask your physician about the policies at your local hospitals, and avoid having provisions in your living will that designate a code status of DNR.

Other Codes Status Designations to Avoid in Your Living Will

No Code

Although a No Code is basically the same as a DNR order, the term No Code is too vague to be useful and can be confusing to health care workers. The same problems that arise from using DNR as a code status will arise with the designation No Code, and so that this status designation is best avoided as well.

Do Not Intubate (DNI)

Patients who ask not to be intubated, which refers to having a breathing tube placed in their throats, are asking not to be placed on a ventilator for the long term. Unfortunately, health care workers may believe the Do Not Intubate (DNI) designation means you have made an informed choice not to be intubated for any reason. If you are drafting a living will, you should be aware of the confusion that may arise from instructions about being intubated or placed on a ventilator.

In fact, many misconceptions exist about being placed on a ventilator. You may think that once you are placed on a ventilator, you will remain attached to it for the rest of your life. This conjures thoughts of lying in a hospital bed for years, being kept alive by artificial means. However, the truth is that if you are placed on the ventilator, you are not likely to be connected to it for a lengthy period of time. You may need the ventilator for only a matter of days, and the breathing tube will be removed when you are able to breathe without assistance.

Often, the patient's fear of depending on a ventilator forever, or the doctor's wish to avoid having to take the patient off a ventilator will lead to use of the DNI option. You should bear in mind that the time you need to be on a ventilator may be brief. If you have chronic lung disease, such as emphysema, long-standing asthma, or congestive heart failure, it may be more difficult for you to be removed from the ventilator; but, it's possible that you may not require it at some point. Should a ventilator become a long-term medical intervention, it may be withdrawn if you so designate this in your living will.

Chemical Code

A Chemical Code means that a patient wants to be treated with medications only. In some hospitals, this means that no other procedures— CPR, insertion of tubes, invasive procedures, or other therapies—are to be used. The problem with this approach is that most medications cannot be given to the patient effectively without using these procedures. For example, a number of medications cannot be circulated through the body without CPR. Many more medications can be given to a patient only intravenously, and the insertion of an intravenous line is considered an invasive procedure since it involves entering a vein with a needle. The Chemical Code seriously limits the usefulness of medications, and it creates a conflict if you request the use of medications but refuse all the procedures needed to give them to you.

Slow Code

The term Slow Code is used among some health care workers to describe situations when it is easier to delay treatment than to determine what level of treatment the patient wants. The Slow Code is often applied to patients who do not appear to benefit from medical care, such as patients of very advanced age, patients with several serious medical problems, and patients with chronic terminal illness. For patients with a Slow Code designation, health care workers will provide the most superficial levels of care, predicting that the patient will die before questions about their health care wishes arise. Using very specific terms in your living will and making sure that your wishes are well known can prevent you from becoming a victim of the Slow Code.

Real Life Examples

To help you understand how code status works in the real world and to emphasize how important it is that you and your loved ones completely understand the concept of these codes, following are real-life stories of patients facing life-threatening emergencies.

Case E

An eighty-three-year-old female patient was brought to the emergency room after a fall. She complained of left knee pain and dizziness. The patient had an X-ray and an EKG (heart tracing) performed. The X-ray revealed no broken bones, but the heart tracing revealed a lethal condition called complete heart block (CHB). In complete heart block the electrical pathways in the heart are blocked, which results in the heart beating incorrectly; this can quickly result in death if not corrected. The treatment for this condition is the implantation of a pacemaker.

Controversy ensued among the treating physicians over whether to implant a pacemaker since the patient's nursing home records indicated she was a DNR. Pacemakers, although easily placed are expensive, and the initial treating cardiologist concluded that placing one was not justified in a patient who was a DNR. However, after long discussions with the physicians and family, a pacemaker was implanted. The woman left the hospital to rejoin her family and lived comfortably in their care for a number of years.

The physicians involved handled this case appropriately. Based on the patient's code status, the doctors treating her were to withhold treatment only if she was in cardiac arrest. The patient had not entered cardiac arrest, and her condition could be treated with a pacemaker.

Case F

A seventy-five-year-old man had prostate cancer that had spread throughout his body. He had stopped chemotherapy and radiation treatment and enrolled in Hospice Care. One night, when he developed a fever, his wife called his doctor but spoke to the on-call doctor instead. Although the patient was enrolled in Hospice Care, the on-call doctor sent him to the emergency room, where the patient's breathing became worse. Not knowing the patient's code status, health care workers treated him as a Full Code and placed him on a ventilator.

When the patient's family arrived, they told health care workers that the patient was enrolled in Hospice Care. Health care workers apologized to the family and explained that the patient was treated as a Full Code because they had no other information on him. The family asked that the patient be removed from the ventilator. After support was withdrawn, the patient was given medications to make him comfortable, and he died surrounded by his loved ones.

In this case, the family correctly provided the man's living will, but only after he had been sent to the emergency room. The on-call doctor should not have sent the patient to the emergency room at all, and he should certainly not have done so without telling health care workers the patient's code status. The patient's wife should also have taken additional measures to tell health care workers that her husband was in Hospice Care.

You can avoid a situation similar to this one by having a living will that clearly communicates your code status to all health care personnel and to your loved ones.

You should also discuss your wishes in depth with your family.

Case G

A forty-one-year-old woman had breast cancer that had spread to her lungs. She wore an oxygen mask but was able to live at home with her family. She went to the emergency room because she was having trouble breathing. Her condition became worse, and health care workers determined that she needed to be placed on a ventilator.

Health care workers asked the family whether the woman had a living will. The family had never discussed the patient's health care wishes, so they couldn't answer the question. They also didn't know whether anyone had discussed Hospice Care with the patient or what her preference would have been. Health care workers asked the family what measures the patient would have wanted in a life-threatening situation. The shocked family members could not answer.

Because immediate action had to be taken, and they had no information to guide them, health care workers presumed that the patient was a Full Code. The patient was placed on the ventilator. Two days later, the family decided to withdraw life support measures, and the patient died.

Is your family able to tell health care workers what your code status is? Do they know what your health care wishes are? The importance of making these points clear cannot be overstated.

Problem: Living Wills Are Not Individualized

Many living wills are not tailored to the needs of each individual patient. Living will forms and other templates can rob you of the chance to select individual treatments and record your specific wishes. This lack of specifics can create problems when health care personnel try to determine your code status or your treatment instructions. Many of these boilerplate forms—available on the Internet, from social service agencies, or from an attorney's office—are not created with a physician's input. They don't contain language or address situations that would be familiar to the health care workers who must read and understand your living will.

Boilerplate living wills may leave out entire classes of treatments, and they usually do not address code status at all. These poorly written or incomplete forms force health care workers to rely only on your health care proxy, if you have one, or to turn to your loved ones, who may not be ready or able to address their questions.

Problem: Lack of Informed Consent

Another potential problem with living wills is a lack of informed consent. Informed consent means that you understand all the risks and benefits involved with your decisions as well as the effects your decisions will have on you.

If you are admitted to a hospital and you have not created a living will, federal law requires the hospital to provide you with information about living wills. They may offer you a "generic" form. However, it is almost impossible to obtain informed consent in that situation because you don't have the opportunity to study the form or the options it offers you. You would essentially be signing it under pressure and without informed consent.

The best approach is to speak with your doctor about a living will before an emergency arises. However, be aware that you may need to be proactive and request a conference to discuss this subject. Although physicians have a legal and moral responsibility under the doctrine of informed consent, they often spend little or no time discussing different types of treatment and alternatives with patients. There are several possible reasons for such lack of communication between physicians and patients.

Physicians may feel they do not have adequate time, and they may feel they are not compensated for their efforts.

- They may want to avoid causing pain and being the bearer of bad news.
- They may lack knowledge of advance directive laws and training in how to deliver bad news.
- They may view death as an enemy to be defeated.
- They may anticipate a disagreement with the patient and/or family.
- They may have legal concerns and feel threatened by such discussions.

Whatever the reason for a physician's reluctance to talk with you about the choices in your living will and what they will mean to you, it is imperative that you ask any and all questions you need to have answered to make informed decisions.

The following case study emphasizes the importance of having a living will and having the treatment terms used in it explained so you are clear about their meaning, benefits, risks, and possible alternatives.

Case H

A fifty-four-year-old male, who was diagnosed with an advanced form of lung cancer, arrived at an emergency room with trouble breathing. The patient had been told that he had at most a year to live. It was obvious at first sight that this patient was experiencing an acute life-threatening event and that he needed to be placed on a ventilator.

The patient was in such distress that he could not answer questions appropriately. His wife was asked if her husband had an advance directive. Her answer was no. She was then asked if they had ever discussed life support issues. Again her answer was no. The patient's wife then produced a brochure that was given to her on a previous hospital visit. She said she did not understand the information it contained, stating over and over that the contents had not been explained to her. She was then offered two options. The first was to put an endotracheal tube (breathing tube) into her husband's windpipe and place him on a ventilator. This would allow her time to cope, as well as to discuss the severity of the situation with the rest of her family. The second option would be to do nothing except make him comfortable and allow him to die. The first option was chosen, and three days later the family decided to withdraw all life support and the patient died.

Unfortunately, no one had explained advance directives to the patient or his family, or the benefits of Hospice Care. After his original diagnosis, this patient and his family had no idea what was to come over the course of the next year. They were not prepared to answer the vital questions they would eventually be asked. Had they been prepared, the patient's death, although painful for the family, could have been less traumatic for them.

Even when patients do discuss living wills with their physicians, confusion can still arise, particularly when the patient does not fully understand the information given. The following case study demonstrates this point.

Case 1

A seventy-year-old female patient with chronic lung disease, resulting from a long history of smoking, became short of breath and went to the emergency room. While in the ER, the patient had a chest X-ray that showed pneumonia. Her breathing worsened and she required endotracheal intubation (a breathing tube) and ventilation (a breathing machine). When the patient was advised of the treatment recommendation, she noted that she had been told by her doctor never to be put on a breathing machine for fear of requiring it for the rest of her life.

The patient was informed that a treatable condition such as pneumonia should not require long-term dependency on the ventilator. Likewise, her condition was in the beginning stages of chronic lung disease, and she was currently using only an inhaler and did not require oxygen at home.

However, to honor the misinformed patient's wishes, health care workers first treated her with mask-type oxygen devices. These treatments were unsuccessful and she subsequently had to be placed on a ventilator. After agreeing to this course of treatment, she quickly recovered and was removed from the ventilator in two days.

It is important to have a living will in place before a life-threatening emergency occurs. It is also important that you and your health care proxy have informed consent—that you clearly understand the provisions of the living will.

3

When Does a Living Will Become Active?

Your living will becomes *effective* when you complete it and have it signed and witnessed in accordance with your state requirements. However, saying that the living will is effective means only that it is legally binding. It is not *active*. Your living will—or most importantly, the medical treatments you wish to receive—will become active only if your condition becomes terminal and you're unable to state your wishes or if you enter a persistent vegetative state. As long as a patient is able to make healthcare decisions, the living will cannot be used.

Although there is no connection between a living will and a last will and testament, it may be helpful to examine an analogy between the two in terms of how a legal document becomes active. Once you sign your last will and testament, the will becomes effective. However, that does not give your family the right to come to your home and take your property and other assets, nor does it mean the person you chose as an executor would begin his or her duties to divide your estate. Before your will becomes active and the directions in it can be followed, you must be deceased.

Similarly, before anyone can actually use the list of selected treatments in your living will, you must be in a persistent vegetative state or in a terminal condition and unable to communicate with others. If you can communicate, you can tell health care workers what you want, and no one needs to turn to the living will or your health care proxy.

Patient Self-Determination Act

On November 5, 1990, Congress passed the Patient Self-Determination Act (PSDA). It became effective on December 1, 1991. The PSDA affects many Medicare and Medicaid providers such as hospitals, nursing homes, hospice programs, home health agencies, and HMOs. It requires them to give adult individuals, at the time of inpatient admission or enrollment, certain information about their rights under state laws governing advance directives, including:

- the right to participate in and direct their own health care decisions

- the right to accept or refuse medical or surgical treatment

- the right to prepare an advance directive

The act also requires that patients be given information on the provider's policies that govern the utilization of these rights. It also prohibits institutions from discriminating against a patient who does not have an advance directive. The PSDA further requires institutions to document patient information and provide ongoing community education on advance directives.

What Is a Terminal Condition?

A terminal condition is any health condition that does not respond to sound medical treatment and will result in a patient's death. The definition of "sound medical treatment" may differ from state to state, but in a very general way, it means that your physician is using his or her judgment as a professional to treat the condition.

In most states, two physicians are required to document that your condition is terminal or that you are in a persistent vegetative state. You may want to structure your living will so that one of these physicians is your primary care physician and the other be a doctor who specializes in the condition affecting you. Together, they will decide whether available treatments would only prolong death without improving the chances of your regaining health.

It's also important to remember that if you are still able to communicate with those around you, your living will is not activated—even if your condition is terminal.

What Is a Persistent Vegetative State?

According to the National Institute of Neurological Disorders and Stroke, people in a persistent vegetative state are not aware of their surroundings and have lost the ability to think. They still have a normal sleep pattern and are able to breathe and circulate fluids throughout the body normally. They may make faces, cry, or even laugh, but they can't speak or respond to commands. They may open their eyes, but they cannot learn or remember things.

A persistent vegetative state is often the result of a metabolic injury. Advanced kidney failure and problems caused by a lack of oxygen to your brain are two examples of metabolic problems; they both damage the chemical processes necessary for your body to work properly.

If you are in a permanent vegetative state, and two doctors determine that treatment would only prolong the process of your dying, a living will allows them to withhold or withdraw treatment.

Stabilization First

Because your living will is activated only by your being terminally ill or in a persistent vegetative state, in an emergency situation it should have no bearing on your initial care and stabilization in a hospital. If you enter a hospital emergency room, before health care workers do anything else, they will try to stabilize your condition. They will provide the treatment necessary to stop your condition from worsening. They will stop you from bleeding or help you to breathe if necessary. In short, they're trying to save your life. There are a number of reasons that immediate treatment is the wisest decision at the outset, even before health care workers refer to your living will.

First, health care workers are working within the "golden hour," which is your first sixty minutes in the hospital. During this hour, which may be extended to ninety minutes in some cases, health care workers have their best chance of successfully treating the medical problems that brought you to the hospital. Second, any delay resulting while care workers determine your code status may compromise your treatment. You'll recall that the delay in treating patients who were wrongly believed to have DNR orders was sometimes life-threatening. By immediately trying to stabilize you, health care providers eliminate that delay, and you have the best chance of survival.

Third, when health care workers stabilize you, they give family members more time to arrive at the hospital;

then, if necessary, your family can be gathering your living will and health care power of attorney, notifying your health care proxy, and reviewing your wishes. The effort to stabilize you as soon as you arrive basically buys your loved ones time to put your wishes into action.

"A lifesaving intervention can always be withdrawn later. But it's important to stabilize the patient first, while determining which course of treatment is best."
—Dr. Ferdinando Mirarchi

Finally, treatments to save your life can always be withdrawn later. But the risk of delaying treatments to patients who do want them—and remember, everyone is initially presumed to want them—is too great to justify not stabilizing patients as soon as they arrive.

Ideally, your living will would work for you as well as it did for the following patient and her family as the patient approached the end of her life.

Case J

An eighty-two-year-old woman was found at home, unresponsive, two hours after a dinner party with her son. She had a past medical history of high blood pressure and high cholesterol. The son found her and was unable to awaken her, so he summoned a paramedic by calling 911. When the paramedic arrived, they asked what happened and also asked if the patient had a living will. The son said she did and provided a copy to the paramedic.

She was taken to the emergency room. The paramedic and the son brought the woman's living will to the attention of the emergency department physician who, after reviewing it, placed the patient on a ventilator. A CAT scan of the patient's brain showed a large bleeding stroke.

A neurosurgeon was consulted to evaluate her and the findings of the CAT scan. The neurosurgeon felt that this was a nonsurvivable bleeding stroke. At that time, the emergency department physician discussed the findings with the son and recommended withdrawing life support. Health care providers then utilized her living will to withdraw care and support and allow nature to take its course.

Several important points are made by this case study. First, the actions taken by both medical personnel and family members demonstrate how a living will is intended to be used. Initial care should never be delayed due to a living will because a physician does not always know how a patient might respond after treatment begins. It is far better to administer treatment and later withdraw it rather than regret not implementing treatment immediately. Also, as shown in this case study, often a second physician is required by state law to confirm a terminal illness.

Unfortunately, when a number of physicians disagree in their interpretation of a living will, the results can be fatal, as shown in the next case study.

Case K

A sixty-year-old male with high blood pressure, diabetes, and cardiac disease was seen in the emergency department for chest pain. He was asked if he had a living will, which he did, and he provided a copy for the records. His blood work and EKG looked acceptable, but it was recommended that he be admitted to the hospital for more testing. When the emergency medicine physician contacted the patient's primary physician for admission, the primary care physician asked why the patient needed to be admitted to the hospital. The ER doctor said he needed to be admitted because he had chest pain; the ER doctor was concerned it could be his heart. In fact, the ER doctor asked the patient whether he would he be willing to undergo a heart catheterization if it was needed and the patient emphatically said yes. The primary care physician then said that the patient had a living will and did not need to be admitted to the hospital because the patient was a DNR. The ER doctor then reviewed the living will again and insisted the patient be admitted to the hospital and be considered a candidate for a heart catheterization.

The primary care physician then finally agreed to admit the patient to the hospital and gave instructions to his nurse to do so. The nurse asked for the diagnosis. It was chest pain. The nurse asked for a code status and was told by the primary care physician that it was DNR. When the nurse asked the doctor if he would like cardiology to be consulted, the doctor said, "Why? He is a DNR."

Four hours later the patient was in his hospital room and the chest pain returned. He began to feel sweaty and faint and then passed out. The heart monitor showed that he was in cardiac arrest. A code blue was called, and hospital personnel responded. The physician who was to lead the resuscitation quickly looked at the man's chart and saw a living will with a DNR order. He canceled the code blue. The patient died.

The living will should have had no bearing on this patient's treatment because he was not terminal, nor was he in a persistent vegetative state. This patient should have been aggressively treated with medications immediately but was not because his primary care physician felt the living will instructed that he should not be resuscitated. Treating his condition aggressively would have more than likely prevented the patient's cardiac arrest. When the man did develop a cardiac arrest, he should have been aggressively treated. But he was not because the physician in charge looked at his living will and he, too, misinterpreted it to mean DNR, despite the patient having a clear cause for his condition that may have been successfully treated.

Suspending Your Living Will

You should know that, under certain circumstances, your living will may not be honored. For example, if you are not terminally ill and have surgery, your living will may be suspended during the operation and for several days afterwards to give the surgery maximum opportunity to be successful.

In addition, many states have statutes that prevent withholding or withdrawing treatment from a pregnant woman who may be permanently unconscious or dying. The rationale is that she should be kept alive until the fetus can be delivered.

If you intend to be an organ donor, you need to make the language of your living clear and specific regarding your wishes to donate your organs and include permission to suspend your living will if it interferes with donation of your organs. Otherwise, as demonstrated by the following scenario, having your requests met may be difficult.

Case L

A fifty-year-old male with no previous medical problems developed a headache, later passed out and remained unconscious. Paramedics were called. His wife gave them a copy of his living will. The paramedic reviewed the living will, called the hospital for medical instruction and advised the doctor at the hospital that they were coming in with a fifty-year-old unresponsive DNR patient. The patient required intubation but did not receive that intervention because of the living will. The patient was found to have a ruptured aneurysm in the brain that essentially left him brain dead. It was recommended that care not be instituted and that he be allowed to die. The wife remembered he wished to be an organ donor, and she wanted to pursue this course.

The physician was told by the organ center recovery service that the patient needed to be aggressively treated to avoid damage to the heart and other organs. The physician stated that doing so would be unethical since the living will, he believed, stated the patient's code status was DNR. This situation raised controversy and debate over ethics and legalities. Attorneys and the hospital administration, among others, were involved. Finally, after a long delay, the patient's organs were procured; unfortunately, there was potential that his organs had been damaged due to the long waiting time prior to the initiation of treatment.

In this scenario, the issue of instituting initial care should never have come up. The patient should have been aggressively treated immediately. However, the paramedics' actions demonstrated that they misinterpreted the living will as a DNR and DNR was misunderstood to mean "Do Not Treat."

The physician caring for the patient in the emergency room should have realized the patient was a full code and instituted care. But due to the structure of the living will, the doctor also misinterpreted the document as a DNR. This patient should have received aggressive stabilization prior to getting to the emergency room and at the very least should have been aggressively treated in the emergency room.

To avoid this problem, information and direction about organ donation should be listed in your living will. Specifically, it should state that the living will is to be suspended in the event that organs need to be procured. Instructions could even state that the patient can be transferred to a transplant facility, which has a "non-beating heart" program; under such a program, organs can be removed shortly after the heart has stopped. This action minimizes the risk of tissue damage to the organs. If this directive is placed in the document, it should stipulate that health care providers are permitted to take these actions as long as the patient's family will not incur any costs.

When Your Living Will Is Challenged

If you have been clear in your discussion of your wishes with your health care proxy, your physician, and your loved ones, you are not likely to encounter conflicts or disagreements. Sometimes, however, the stress and anxiety caused by changes in your medical condition or the reality of working with a patient's living will can be exhausting. There are cases of loved ones disregarding a patient's stated wishes and asking to have treatment prolonged to avoid the patient's death; in other cases, relatives have asked to have treatment withdrawn in order to hasten the patient's death. In yet other instances, health care proxies, who have been appointed to make health care decisions for the patient, have disagreed with the recommendations of the physicians.

To handle such conflicts, an impartial resource such as an ethics consultation may be very helpful. Although they do not make binding decisions, ethics consultants can certainly help the parties involved sort out the points of confusion and encourage discussion of possible solutions. Family and health care proxies should remember they do have a right to request a physician who will honor the wishes of the living will and proxy. In the face of continuing conflict, they may choose to engage the courts, although courts in many states have made public their wish to have these matters resolved privately, rather than in the courtroom.

Reviewing and Updating Your Living Will

Remember that your living will should be revised as your needs and medical condition change. It's a good idea to review your living will every six months and discuss it with your doctor. If you actually change your living will, you will need to sign it and have it notarized or witnessed again. Of course, your health care proxy and your loved ones should also be advised of the changes.

If you don't discuss such updates in your living will, your loved ones and your proxy may be confident they know your wishes, when, in fact, they will be working with outdated information. Reviewing your living will once a year may require uncomfortable discussions more often than you would like. But those discussions will be worthwhile if your loved ones are ever in the position of needing to know your health care wishes in the event of a serious medical emergency. You may wish to pick a day out of the year and review your living will on that date each year.

4

Medical Treatments in Your Living Will

One of the most important components of your living will is the list of medical treatments you do or do not wish to receive. Being familiar with these treatments and understanding them will help you make informed choices in your living will. With this information, you will be better able to have an informed discussion about your health care wishes with your physician and with your loved ones.

Cardiopulmonary Resuscitation (CPR)

Cardiopulmonary resuscitation, or CPR, is a procedure to restore breathing and heartbeat in patients who have no pulse and are not breathing. You may think of CPR as being mouth-to-mouth resuscitation, and in fact the mouth-to-mouth technique is used by emergency technicians in the field; however, in a hospital setting, CPR is accomplished with the placement of an endotracheal tube down the throat along with external chest compressions. Oxygen is moved into the patient's lungs, causing blood to circulate throughout the body, especially to the heart and brain. The procedure is also necessary to properly circulate many medications through the bloodstream. Despite the dramatic depiction of CPR you may have seen on television or in the movies, you should know that most patients have no memory or pain from this lifesaving procedure.

CPR is a fairly basic, often necessary lifesaving technique. However, if you choose Comfort Care or Hospice Care, then you have already decided to reject this intervention or procedure. If you choose Full Code Except Cardiac Arrest, you have chosen to have lifesaving treatment until the time your breathing and heartbeat stop, meaning you will have chosen not to have CPR.

Advanced Cardiac Life Support Protocols

The *advanced cardiac life support protocols* (ACLS) is a set of techniques and medications designed to restore blood pressure and correct or restore the rhythm of your heart. The protocols include the use of certain medications, paired with CPR, to make sure that the medicine is circulated through your body. If you choose to have CPR administered, you should choose this option, too, since the techniques complement each other. If your code status is Full Code Except Cardiac Arrest, you can still choose to have advanced cardiac life support until the time that your heartbeat stops entirely. If you chose Comfort Care or Hospice Care, you have decided against this advanced support.

Endotracheal Intubation

Endotracheal intubation is one way for health care workers to connect you to a mechanical ventilator to help you breathe. To use this method, health care workers will place a plastic tube into your mouth and down your windpipe. This tube is connected to a ventilator. Endotracheal intubation is a common procedure and is often used during surgery to help a patient under general anesthesia to breathe properly.

It is important for you to understand that, in the case of a life-threatening emergency, being connected to a ventilator is often a temporary process. You may be connected to the ventilator just for a matter of hours or days before your condition improves enough for you to breathe on your own, at which time the tube is removed.

If you are willing to be placed on a ventilator temporarily in case of an emergency, you'll want your living will to state this. You can choose to be connected to the ventilator even if you have not stopped breathing entirely, so this is an option for patients who choose Full Code Except Cardiac Arrest. Patients who choose Comfort Care or Hospice Care have decided against being connected to a ventilator.

Long-Term Mechanical Ventilation

Patients on long-term mechanical ventilation may regain the ability to breathe on their own, and at that point, they would be disconnected from the machine.

However, if your condition worsens, the fact you have chosen this option does not consign you to a lifetime of mechanical ventilation. If it becomes unlikely that you will be able to breathe without the help of the machine, your living will can be reviewed or your health care proxy can be consulted. At that time, the decision can be made to keep you connected to the ventilator or to be removed from it, in keeping with your wishes.

If you are connected to the ventilator for a longer period of time, you will probably have a *tracheotomy*. In this procedure, you will be placed under anesthesia, and a very small incision will be made in your neck, allowing the insertion of a narrow tube directly into your windpipe. If you are a Comfort Care or Hospice Care patient, you have decided against long-term mechanical ventilation. Other patients should remember that this measure, although it is long term, may or may not be permanent. You should also remember that if the situation worsens, your proxy can express your wishes to be removed from the ventilator.

Defibrillation

Defibrillation is the use of an electric shock to restore the rhythm of your heartbeat. The shock is usually delivered through a paddle or pad that is placed on your chest. Health care workers may also use a set of pads to deliver the shock. Of all the medical treatments described here, this is the only one of proven value in restoring the heart's normal beating.

You should know that defibrillation in the real world is not like the process often shown on television. You will probably not be jolted up off the bed, and you most likely will not remember the experience at all once you regain consciousness. Television uses dramatic license in its depiction of many emergency procedures; these procedures are rarely as dramatic in real life.

If you choose Comfort Care or Hospice Care, you have decided against defibrillation. If you are a Full Code Except Cardiac Arrest, and you want to have the rhythm of your heartbeat restored unless it has stopped beating completely, you can still decide to have defibrillation. Such a decision does not conflict with Full Code Except Cardiac Arrest.

If your heart has stopped beating entirely, you may have entered a stage called asystole, and defibrillation will not be used; at this stage, the heart has no electrical activity, is not pumping any blood, and will not respond to defibrillation.

Invasive Procedures

Before making decisions about invasive procedures, you should understand more about what an invasive procedure really is. The category of invasive procedures includes a wide variety of treatments, ranging from a simple intravenous drip to surgery. Intravenous drips in the arm or leg can provide lifesaving medications. If your lung collapses, a tube can be inserted into your chest to reinflate the lung. These and many other medical treatments cannot be delivered effectively without the use of an invasive procedure.

Remember that when you are in surgery, health care workers will temporarily lift the restrictions you established in your living will. The primary reason for this is that the many forms of life support you have chosen (or not chosen) will already have been instituted when you undergo surgery. For example, if you have chosen Full Code Except Cardiac Arrest, and you enter surgery as part of your treatment, if during the course of your surgery your heart stops beating, doctors will attempt to restore your heartbeat. Once the surgery is completed, your living will again takes precedence.

Invasive Emergency Procedures

This category of procedures includes emergency surgery, insertion of chest tubes, intravenous delivery of lifesaving medications, and other invasive procedures intended to save lives. If you chose Full Code or Full Code Except Cardiac Arrest, you have decided to choose in favor of invasive emergency procedures. Even for patients who choose Full Code Except Cardiac Arrest, many of these invasive procedures can be used until the time the patient enters cardiac arrest, with the exception of emergency surgery. If you choose Comfort Care or Hospice Care, you have decided against invasive emergency procedures.

Invasive Comfort Procedures

This category includes invasive procedures intended to relieve a patient's pain and anxiety. Even the use of a central intravenous line can be a comfort procedure because it allows health care workers to draw blood samples without having to repeatedly make needle sticks. Pain medications can also be delivered through an intravenous drip, and even some surgical procedures can be used to make patients more comfortable. Comfort Care patients can choose this option, which will allow doctors to make them comfortable without performing procedures that will extend or save their life. All other patients can choose this option if they want health care workers to be able to relieve pain or anxiety through the use of invasive procedures.

Intravenous Fluids

A temporary treatment, intravenous fluids are usually based on a saline solution, or a saline solution mixed with sugar. The fluids can be used to help keep you hydrated if you cannot drink water, and they are a convenient way to deliver medications, including pain medications. If your condition does not improve, the option to withdraw treatment is available.

If you choose Comfort Care or Hospice Care, you can choose not to have intravenous fluids administered, and your pain medications will be delivered in another way.

Intravenous Antibiotics

Intravenous antibiotics prevent or kill infection and are usually delivered into a vein in the arm or hand through an intravenous line; they can also be given through a central line, which is a special intravenous line that is inserted into a large vein in the neck or leg. Not only can medications be given through this line, but blood can be drawn without multiple needle sticks.

Health care workers prefer to give you antibiotics in the form of pills whenever possible, and they will work to improve your condition so that you will be able to take pills. Intravenous antibiotics are, therefore, a temporary option in most cases. Comfort Care and Hospice Care patients will likely turn down this measure, but all others will want to allow for intravenous antibiotics administered as a basic medical treatment option.

Organ Donation

If you have already made a decision about organ donation, indicating this on your living will is a way for you to tell health care workers the specifics of your decision. Without this information in your living will, medical staff will need to locate your organ donor card. It's important that your instructions stated in your living will are the same as those on your organ donor card and on your driver's license.

Your family should also be aware of your decision. If you have not yet decided whether being an organ donor is right for you, a great deal of information on organ donation is available to help you make this important choice. You'll find a reference to a Web site with information about organ donation in the Resources section of this book.

Medical science now allows for transplants of many body parts and organs. You may be aware of transplants for hearts, kidneys, and livers, but you may not know that cornea transplants can restore sight to blind people, or that bone and bone marrow can be transplanted. Even tendons, ligaments, the tissue that connect muscle to bones, can be transplanted. Your organs can be a life-saving gift to those awaiting a transplant.

There are some misconceptions about organ donation. Some people mistakenly believe that if they are organ donors, health care workers may not try as hard to save their lives. Others think that health care workers may even try to bring about their deaths in order to harvest their organs, or that their organs will be taken before they die. Others believe that they are too old to become organ donors. All these beliefs are untrue. Your status as an organ donor has no effect on the level of care you receive, and no organ would ever be harvested without your consent. Finally, your age does not disqualify you as an organ donor. However, your doctor can tell you whether you have health conditions that might disqualify you from being a donor.

If you do not want to be an organ donor, you should make sure that your family knows and that your driver's license reflects the fact. In addition, you should document such a wish in your living will. If you are willing to donate only certain organs or if you want to donate only in some situations (for example, only for your family members or only to save a life), you can put this choice on your living will. Your family can choose to offer your organs after death if you have not stated in writing that they are not to do so.

Long-Term Total Parenteral Nutrition

Parenteral nutrition is a form of nutrition that is delivered into a vein, through an intravenous line, rather than through the digestive system. It is an effective way to receive nutrients if part of your digestive system is injured. Although this is considered a long-term measure, it is usually a temporary one, intended to last only for a period of weeks or months. For example, if your intestine was blocked, you could receive nutrition in this way until the blockage was removed with surgery. Remember that if your health condition worsens and you are unable to make decisions, your loved ones and your health care proxy can be consulted about whether you would want to continue with this process or have it withdrawn.

Feeding Tube

A *feeding tube* is a way to provide nutrition to patients who have lost their ability to swallow or chew food. A feeding tube, which is surgically inserted, allows nutritional supplements to be delivered directly into the stomach.

A feeding tube is also intended to be a temporary measure only. You can choose to have the feeding tube implanted through a simple, invasive procedure, and then arrange to have the tube withdrawn if your condition does not improve. As with other changes in your condition, your health care proxy would be consulted about the steps to be taken if there was any change in your condition. If you are in a persistent vegetative state, you would not be aware of the withdrawal of the feeding tube. As your body is deprived of nutrition, substances would build up in the bloodstream to naturally reduce discomfort until a chemical imbalance eventually caused a fatal loss of rhythm in the your heartbeat.

Thrombolytic Medications and Angioplasty

A *thrombolytic* medication is one that dissolves blood clots, and it is often used in patients who have clots that are restricting blood flow to the heart, lungs, or brain. *Angioplasty* is a surgical procedure in which a tiny balloon is inserted into a blood vessel and inflated to open a blockage. These measures can be lifesaving, especially for patients who have had a heart attack or who are recovering from one.

If you are a Comfort Care patient or enrolled in Hospice Care, you would not want to choose this option. If you choose Full Code or Full Code Except Cardiac Arrest, you *would* choose this option; thrombolytic medications and angioplasty can be used to prevent cardiac arrest.

Blood and Blood Products

You are probably already aware of the ways surgeons use blood for transfusions during surgical procedures; however, you may not realize that blood and blood components are versatile and very useful in other medical treatments. For example, white blood cells can be given to you to help fight infections. Blood platelets can help control bleeding by helping a patient's normal formation of clots. If you are hospitalized, you are very likely to need blood or blood products at one time or another, but health care workers will not give you blood or blood products unless they are absolutely necessary.

You may be worried about the risks of contracting hepatitis, HIV, or other blood-borne diseases through the use of blood or blood products. Although such risks have not been completely eliminated, modern screening practices have greatly reduced these risks. You face a greater risk from complications of your own medical condition than from any diseases carried with blood.

Comfort Care and Hospice Care patients would decide against using blood and blood products, which would be used to save or prolong life. Other patients will probably elect to use blood and blood products as part of their treatment.

If your religious beliefs cause you to reject the use of blood or blood products as part of your medical or healing treatment, you can choose not to use them. To further assist health care workers who read your living will, you should include any stipulations about religious beliefs that prevent you from receiving blood and blood products.

Hemodialysis and Peritoneal Dialysis

If your kidneys have failed, your body is unable to remove waste products from the blood stream. *Hemodialysis* involves the use of a machine to clean wastes from the blood after the kidneys have failed. The blood travels through tubes to a dialyzer, which is a machine that removes wastes and extra fluid. The cleaned blood then goes back into the body. Patients are typically connected to the dialysis machine for a few hours per session.

Another method of removing wastes from the body is *peritoneal dialysis*. For this procedure, a dialysis solution is placed into your abdomen. Blood flows through the solution, which cleanses the blood, and then the solution is drained from the body. No machine is used in peritoneal dialysis. Dialysis can be a short-term measure, but is often a long-term treatment option; patients on dialysis very often live long lives without compromising their quality of life significantly. It is also possible for dialysis to be a temporary treatment option—for example to reverse kidney failure brought on by a medical condition. The treatment can be withdrawn at any time.

Dialysis is a life-extending process, so if you choose Comfort Care or Hospice Care, you would choose to not have dialysis. You can choose to have dialysis withdrawn at any time. If your condition changes so that you require dialysis on an ongoing basis, your health care proxy can put your wishes into effect after a discussion with your doctor.

Your religious beliefs may cause you to reject dialysis as a medical treatment option; if that's the case, you should indicate that on your living will form.

Implanted Pacemaker and Defibrillator

A *pacemaker* is a small battery-powered device that is placed under the skin in the upper chest and joined to the heart by pacing wires; these wires measure the pulse and correct heart rhythms.

An *implanted defibrillator* is a slightly larger device, also connected directly to your heart. It monitors your heart constantly for irregular heart rhythms that can cause sudden cardiac arrest. If your heart develops an abnormal rhythm, the defibrillator turns itself on to restore the rhythm with an electric pulse, and then the pacemaker backs it up to keep your heart running. Both of these devices can be implanted with a minimally invasive surgery, and they can be turned off at any time using a computer and a magnetic device that does not involve any invasive procedure.

Like conventional defibrillation, this implanted defibrillator begins to work when the heart develops an abnormal rhythm but before it stops entirely. Consequently, this treatment, with a pacemaker backup, can and should be an option if you choose Full Code Except Cardiac Arrest.

For the best information on all these treatments and how they may work with your medical condition and satisfy your health care wishes, you should talk to your physician in order to make an informed choice.

5

Adopting the Medical Living Will with Code Status

If you don't yet have a living will, the time to draft one is now. As stressed throughout this book, having a living will can save you and your family emotional pain and suffering.

This chapter provides instructions for adopting the "Medical Living Will with Code Status," which you will find in Appendix A of this book. This document, developed by Dr. Ferdinando Mirarchi, is intended to ensure patient safety. If you choose to adopt this living will, you are also encouraged to confer with both your attorney and your physician. Earlier in the book, the use of "boilerplate living wills" was discouraged, so why is it okay to use the Medical Living Will with Code Status template? There are several reasons.

- This medical living will is oriented toward medical professionals—those who would be treating you if you were seriously ill.

- This document incorporates your code status designation at the very beginning of the living will, leaving no question in the minds of medical staff and family what your wishes are.

- This living will also lists and explains specific medical interventions, or treatments, that you may or may not wish to receive, depending on the status of your health.

- The list of medical interventions is more encompassing than those listed in traditional living wills.

- This living will insists that a terminal condition be confirmed by the attending physician and one other physician who is a specialist in the condition from which the patient is suffering.

- This living will provides that a patient's case be reviewed by an ethics committee if disagreements should arise between an attending physician and a health care power of attorney over whether to continue measures to prolong the patient's life.

Whether you're a thirty-year-old in excellent health or a ninety-five-year-old with a chronic condition, you can use this document to create an individualized living will that speaks to your specific treatment needs and describes your unique health care requirements. The effort you put into completing this living will can be of great benefit should you require emergency medical treatment; you'll make the experience easier on your loved ones, yourself, and health care personnel.

Confer with Your Physician

If you choose to adopt the Medical Living Will with Code Status desginations or choose to revise your original living will, make sure the document contains appropriate language and provisions. You are encouraged to complete this living will form with the help of your physician.

Also, periodically ask your doctor about new medical treatments and how they will affect you and your current medical condition. Your doctor can also help you better understand how the choices in your living will would be put into action. You also will need to keep your primary care physician informed about your changing health care wishes since this doctor is the one who will be in charge of your care if you have a critical illness.

Meet State Law Requirements

Laws governing living wills differ from state to state. For example, laws vary in how readily treatment may be withdrawn by medical personnel; in some states, these orders require much verification, such as a decision based upon a conference between two physicians, whereas in other states, medical staff may accept such an order with relative ease. It is important to make certain your living will is valid in your state.

Seek Legal Guidance

You can take your completed living will, before it has been signed, to your family attorney or to your estate attorney. The attorney can examine it to be sure that you have identified the correct number of witnesses and met any other requirements under the law. Completing as much of the form as possible before you visit your attorney can reduce the amount of time your lawyer must spend on the form, which may save additional attorney fees. Your lawyer may even have a flat fee that would cover reviewing your living will and health care power of attorney as part of an estate package.

If you do not have an attorney, it is possible to find one for this purpose at low cost or no cost to you. Your state bar association may have a referral system that can connect you to a lawyer with knowledge of living wills or to volunteer attorneys who can examine your living will. There may even be a referral phone line that allows you to ask simple questions about your living will. The American Association of Retired Persons (AARP) offers a Legal Services Network, with low-cost attorney services for its members; it also has a Web page with links to low-cost and no-cost legal resources in your state. The Resources section of this book contains a list of other helpful legal resources.

"When drafting your living will, make sure your understanding of the document matches that of your physician's."
—Dr. Ferdinando Mirarchi

Guidelines for Completing the Medical Living Will with Code Status Designations

In addition to your name and personal information, the living will asks you to list those individuals who are to be contacted in the event of a medical emergency.

People to Contact

- Emergency Contact: Fill in the name and phone number of the person you wish to have contacted in the event of a medical emergency.
- Primary Care Physician: Fill in the name and phone number of the physician who cares for you. It is crucial that this physician knows and understands your predetermined wishes since he or she will be called if you suffer an emergency.

- Health Care Power of Attorney: Complete this section by placing the name and phone number of the individual who is to make health care decisions for you. This is not mandatory, but it is highly recommended.
- Attorney: If you have an attorney who played a part in creating your living will, fill in his or her name and telephone number, so health care professionals will know who to contact if necessary.

Your Code Status

On the very first page of the Medical Living Will with Code Status, you are asked to checkmark your code status. This immediately establishes the level of treatment you wish to receive in a medical emergency.

As stressed throughout this book, your living will should clearly and immediately show the appropriate code status designation so that health care workers can identify it right away, irrespective of an emergency worker's opinion. Knowing and communicating your code status helps ensure you will receive the care you wish to receive when you are at your most vulnerable. If you cannot provide this information and it's not listed in your living will, health care personnel will assess the situation, review your living will, and designate a code status themselves.

Witnesses

These are individuals who witness your signature to the living will. State requirements differ regarding the number of witnesses needed to make the document legal. Most states have restrictions about who can be a witness. For examples, most states will not accept your treating physician or one of your relatives as a witness. Other states also reject creditors as witnesses. Some states require that you and your witnesses sign the living will document in the presence of the notary public. Even if your state does not require certification by a notary public, it's a good idea to have your living will notarized anyway; the document immediately appears more authentic to medical personnel.

Hold Harmless Statement

The Hold Harmless Statement, in Section A, states that the living will reflects your health care wishes and that you will not seek legal action against health care workers or the health care facility for following your wishes. Although most states have laws that specifically recognize living wills as legally binding documents, there are three states that do not (New York, Massachusetts, and Michigan). In these three states, living wills are often used anyway, as long as there is clear and convincing evidence that they are a correct expression of the patient's health care wishes.

In addition, every state has slightly different laws describing what the living will should look like. You may find that your living will was signed in one state, but you are being hospitalized in another. Health care workers will still use your living will as long as they can tell that you signed it with informed consent. This Hold Harmless Statement is meant to allow doctors to carry out your wishes without fear of being sued because they did so. It will also help to prove that this living will expresses your health care wishes.

Section A

This section of the living will contains instructions about which medical treatments you wish to receive. Having specified these wishes will make it more likely that your wishes are honored even under the following circumstances:

- A disagreement between your loved ones and your doctor
- Disagreements among loved ones
- A change in your condition
- Your medical history is not available

By completing the statements in this section on medical treatments, you are protecting your safety and individualizing your living will; this information will help health care professionals avoid misinterpreting your wishes.

Medical History

Completing this section as thoroughly as possible transforms your living will into a medical history reference; health care workers can use this important information to make educated decisions about your treatment. This measure can save precious time, eliminating the need for health care staff to seek records on your past treatments and avoiding asking your loved ones questions that they may not be able to answer. In addition, if you find yourself hospitalized at a time when your primary care physician may be difficult to reach, health care workers can work from the medical history you provide until your complete records become available. Your doctor can help you complete this section, which lists the following:

- Your chronic medical conditions
- Past surgeries
- Medications you currently take
- Drug allergies, if any
- Any implants, such as a joint replacement or a pacemaker

You may also attach an electrocardiogram or cardiac catheterization records to your living will.

Family and Friends Who Know About Your Living Will

The last part of Section A asks you to place a check mark next to those people who know about your living will. It is important that you discuss your living will with family and friends. Health care workers will want to know whether you've created your living will with informed consent. They may seek proof that you fully understood what you were doing when you created it, and the best proof available is a declaration that you have discussed it with family, friends, and medical professionals.

If you have not discussed your living will with anyone, it may be difficult to determine whether you created your living will with informed consent. No one could confirm that your living will is an accurate representation of your health care wishes. Without demonstrated informed consent, there is a risk that health care workers would not respect your living will. There's also the risk that your loved ones would not fully understand your health care wishes, and that lack of understanding could cause conflicts between your loved ones and your doctors. You can minimize these risks by discussing your living will with others.

Section B

This section expresses your wishes for a two-physician conference. It instructs your attending physician and another doctor, a specialist in the condition from which you suffer, to hold or withdraw treatments that are only prolonging the process of your death. The two doctors will work together to make that decision, and it will be made only if you are in a terminal condition or state of permanent unconsciousness and not able to make decisions for yourself.

Most states require at least two doctors to work together in this case, so this section of your living will is meant to provide further assurance that this procedure is being followed. Your loved ones and your health care proxy may also find that the input of two medical professionals reduces the pressure on them. Your loved ones and your proxy will have the best information available, and they will be consulted before any decision is made to ensure that your wishes are being followed.

Finally, this section provides that if your health care power of attorney should disagree with your attending physician over whether life support measures should be stopped, an ethics consultation will be called upon to review the case. This is a unique provision, one not usually found in a traditional living will.

Section C

This section outlines your wishes for Comfort or Hospice Care if you are terminally ill. Again, consult your physician about this section. Place your initials next to the provisions that apply to you. If you have decided on this code status designation, you should agree to all four points listed in the section.

6

The Safe Keeping of
Your Living Will

Part of keeping your living will "safe" is making sure it has been prepared so that it is legal in your state. After you have signed your living will or revised it, making sure it is in accordance with your state law requirements, you will need to discuss it with your loved ones. This discussion is rarely easy, but it is very important that your loved ones know your medical wishes. Having others understand your wishes improves the chances that your wishes will be communicated to health care workers if questions should arise. Remember also that health care personnel will take into account the number of people who know what you want as they determine whether you had informed consent when you made your living will.

Make Sure Loved Ones Can Find
Your Living Will

According to the U.S. Registry of Living Wills, approximately 35 percent of living wills cannot be found when they are needed. When you are discussing your living will with loved ones, be sure to tell them where you keep copies of it. Also, give a copy to your health care proxy. The importance of doing so is demonstrated by the following actual account.

Case M

A seventy-four-year-old female with lung cancer that had spread to bone and the brain had opted not to have any treatment and enrolled in Hospice Care. She had a living will drawn up and discussed it with her physician. She wished to be a DNR and receive nothing other than Comfort Care measures and specifically stated she did not want a feeding tube. She discussed all of this with her family as well.

One evening she became very ill with abdominal pain, nausea, and vomiting. She was taken to an emergency room via ambulance; her family was to meet her there.

She was undergoing evaluation by an emergency room physician and became sicker to the point that she was mentally incompetent. The physician tried to glean information from the family members who at this time were very tearful and distraught.

The physician found that the woman's intestine had ruptured and she had intestinal contents spilling into her abdomen. She needed emergency surgery.

The woman had a living will; however, none of the family members knew where to find her living will. The patient moaned that she did not want the surgery, but the family insisted she be taken to the operating room. They even threatened legal action against the physician and the hospital if surgery was not performed.

It turned out that a son had flown in when he found out about his mother's cancer, and it was he who was forcing the other family members to insist she be taken to surgery. Finally the ER physician told the family that he would not recommend the surgery and had a surgeon give an opinion as well. Surgery was not performed. The woman was placed in a patient room with the family and kept comfortable, until she died as she had wished.

The ER physician was faced with legal action by the son after the patient died, but fortunately the case was dropped.

In this case, the stressful situation could have been alleviated had the patient's family been able to find the woman's living will. The woman's family would have understood their mother's wishes, and the question of major surgery would not have arisen.

Keeping Your Living Will Safe and Available

Keep your living will in a safe place. It's a good idea to keep at least one copy with your last will and testament and other estate papers. Your physician or local medical facility, where you have regular appointments, should also have a copy on file. Your health care proxy should also have a copy.

Some EMS programs train paramedics to search for a living will when they are transporting a patient from home to a hospital. They often check the side of the refrigerator or a drawer in a nightstand. There may come a time when you want your living will to be very accessible to family members or medical personnel, so you should place it in a location where it will be easily found.

Unless you are a high-risk patient traveling away from home, you don't need to carry your living will with you when you travel. You will remember that emergency workers will try to stabilize you as soon as you enter the hospital. In the absence of a living will, health care workers will treat you as if your code status is Full Code, and you will receive the highest and most complete level of care until your stated medical wishes direct health care workers to do otherwise.

Living Will Cards

Since it is not practical to carry a copy of your living will with you, you may wish to carry a Medical Living Will Resuscitation card in your wallet or purse. Such a card states your code status. It can also provide the names and numbers of the people to be contacted in case of an emergency. The card will provide health care workers with enough information to proceed until your living will arrives. You will find copies of the cards in Appendix B; you may photocopy a card on bright-colored paper—pink or yellow—and begin carrying it with you immediately. If you change your living will, remember to change your card.

Commonly Asked Questions about Living Wills

1. What is the difference between an advance directive and a living will?

A living will is a type of advance directive. An advance directive is simply a document that is written in advance.

2. Why should I have a living will?

To make sure your wishes are followed. To relieve loved ones from having to make end-of-life decisions without knowing your wishes. To help your doctors follow your medical wishes. To keep the matter out of court, where it will go if family members or health care personnel cannot resolve disagreements.

3. Am I required by law to have a living will?

No, but hospitals and other health care institutions are required by law to ask you if you have one.

4. What happens if I don't have a living will?

If you don't have a living will and are unable to communicate your wishes for medical treatment, someone else must decide for you. Those who may speak for you include: your health care proxy, your guardian, your spouse, or your adult children. By having a living will prepared in advance, your family is spared the additional emotional trauma of deciding who should speak for you in the midst of an emergency.

5. When should I get a living will?

As soon as you become an adult and are mentally competent. If you become mentally incompetent, it's too late to execute a living will. It's best to have a living will before a medical emergency. Start the process by having a discussion with your loved ones about your wishes for medical care.

6. Can my living will be changed or revoked?

Yes, at any time. You can do this verbally by telling a family member or friend. You can also revise your living will at any time. Your doctor must also be notified since the living will becomes part of your medical record.

7. When is a living will effective?

A living will is valid when you sign it. However, it is enacted or activated only if you become unable to express your own wishes for medical treatment and you are terminally ill or in a persistent vegetative state.

8. What if the directions in my living will are not followed?

Medical personnel are required to follow your wishes. If they don't want to follow your wishes, state law may require that you be moved to a facility that will honor your wishes. In such instances, a health care proxy can be helpful in expressing what you would want.

9. Is my living will effective if I move to another state?

Generally, yes it is still effective; however, it is subject to your new state's laws.

10. Must I have my living will certified by a notary public?

Some states require certification by a notary public; others do not. It's recommended you have a notary public certify your living will to ensure chances of it being considered authentic by health professionals. You are required to have witnesses sign your living will.

11. Why is it important to also have a health care proxy?

If a medical issue, which is not covered under your living will, should arise, your appointed health care proxy could speak on your behalf. You can reappoint a different health care proxy in writing or verbally at any time.

12. What is the difference between a health care power of attorney and a health care proxy?

A health care power of attorney is a legal document, in which you name the person you wish to make medical decisions if you become unable to make decisions yourself. The person you name is said to hold health care power of attorney. This person is sometimes referred to as a health care proxy. However, in some circles, a health care proxy is also considered a document—a health care power of attorney. The multiple meanings of these terms can be confusing.

13. Whom should I choose as a health care proxy?

You can name whomever you wish; however, the person must agree to be your proxy. He or she should be someone with whom you are comfortable and whom you trust to make decisions for you if you are incapacitated. Most state laws prohibit some individuals from being health care proxies, including medical personnel or government agencies that handle finances related to your health care.

Appendix A

Consult your physician and attorney to finalize any living will.
This document is not a substitute for an attorney or an attending physician.

Medical Living Will with Code Status
Advance Directive

Name: _____

Phone: _____

Address: _____

City _____State ___Zip Code _____

In an emergency, contact: _____

Phone: _____

Primary Care Physician: _____

Phone: _____

Health Care Power of Attorney: _____

Phone: _____

Attorney: _____

Phone: _____

Please honor these Code Status Designations:

(   )**"Full Code"**

I would like to receive all lifesaving and supportive measures should an emergency arise. Should my condition fail to improve and I am no longer able to make my own decisions, then I would like my advance directive to become active and be followed. Please see sections A and B.

(   ) **"Full Code Except Cardiac Arrest"**

If I suffer from a cardiac arrest, you are not to institute CPR.

(   ) **"Comfort Care/Hospice Care"**

Please see Section C.

Patient Signature: _____Date: _____

Witness Signature #1: _____Date: _____

Witness Signature #2 _____Date: _____

Health Care Power of Attorney Signature: _____

Date: _____

Section A
Hold Harmless Statement

I am aware that state laws vary with respect to advance directive and living wills. These are my wishes with respect to my care. Neither you, nor your health care facility, is to be held responsible, in any way, for following my wishes.

1. I __do __do not   want cardiopulmonary resuscitation.

2. I __do __do not   want advanced cardiac life support protocols to be followed.

3. I __do __do not   want endotracheal intubation.

4. I __do __do not   want long-term mechanical ventilation.

5. I __do __do not   want defibrillation.

6. I __do __do not   want invasive procedures to be performed in an emergency situation.

7. I __do __do not   want invasive procedures to be performed if they will add to my comfort.

8. I __do __do not   want intravenous fluids.

9. I __do __do not   want antibiotics.

10. I __do __do not   want my organs to be donated.

11. I __do __do not   want long-term total parenteral nutrition.

12. I __do __do not   want a feeding tube.

13. I __do __do not   want thrombolytics agents (clot busters) or angioplasty, should it be needed.

14. I __do __do not   want blood or blood products.

15. I __do __do not   want peritoneal or hemodialysis.

16. I __do __do not   wish to have an ethics consultation settle controversy between my treating physician and healthcare power of attorney

Section A (continued)

17. Medical History. My chronic medical conditions and previous surgeries are:

a. _____ f._____ k. _____
b._____ g._____ l _____
c._____ h._____ m._____
d. _____ l._____ n. _____
e. _____ j._____ o. _____

18. Medications. My routine medications are:

a. _____ f._____ k. _____
b._____ g._____ L. _____
c._____ h._____ m._____
d. _____ l._____ n. _____
e. _____ j._____ o. _____

19. Drug Allergies. My known drug allergies are:

a. _____ f._____ k. _____
b._____ g._____ l. _____
c._____ h._____ m._____
d. _____ l. _____ n. _____
e. _____ j. _____ o. _____

_____I have no known allergies to medications.

20. I __do __do not have a copy of an electrocardiogram enclosed.

21. I __do __do not have a copy of a cardiac catheterization enclosed.

22. List any implants such as: joints, lenses for cataracts, pacemaker, or heart valves. List manufacturer name and model number if available.

a._____ b._____ c. _____
d._____ e._____ f._____
g._____ h._____ l._____

23. Please check all with whom you've discussed your living will and wishes for medical treatment.

   a. _____Family   b._____Spiritual Adviser

   c. _____Family Physician   d. _____Physician Specialist

   e. _____Friend   f. _____Attorney

   g. _____No One

Section B

I direct my attending physician, in conjunction with another physician who is a specialist in my life-ending condition, to withhold or withdraw life-sustaining measures that serve only to prolong the process of my dying. I give this permission if I am in a state of permanent unconsciousness and am no longer able to make my own decisions.

Section C
Comfort/Hospice Care

1. In the event that my condition becomes such that I need any emergency or life-sustaining interventions, you are not to institute them. If you have instituted life-saving care without the knowledge of my advance directive, you do have my permission to withdraw such interventions. Initials _____.

2. I have decided that I would like comfort measures and if eligible, Hospice Care only. Initials _____.

3. I would like to be kept comfortable and free from pain to the best of your abilities. Should I become addicted to such medications or should my breathing stop secondary to this intervention, you in no way are to be held responsible. I take full responsibility. Initials _____.

4. I would not want to be transferred to the emergency room for treatment unless you are unable to control my pain where I am currently located. Initials _____.

My Notes:

IN WITNESS WHEREOF, this living will has been executed on this _____ day of _____, 20___, as my free and voluntary act, and I state I am over 18 years of age.

_____
your name

    I, the undersigned, a Notary Public authorized to administer oaths in the State of_____, certify that_____,

                                                                                 your name

having appeared before me and having been first duly sworn, then declared to me that he/she willingly signed and executed this trust agreement and that he/she executed such instrument as his/her free and voluntary act for the purposes therein expressed.

IN WITNESS WHEREOF, I have hereunto subscribed my name and affixed my official seal this ___ day of _____, 20___

_____

Notary Public
Seal of Notary Public

Appendix B

Medical Living Will Cards

Choose the card that fits your needs and photocopy on bright-color paper. Fill in your name and details and carry the card with you. You may wish to list the medications you take on the reverse side of the card. As mentioned earlier, if you change your living will, you should also change the card.

My Medical Living Will
Resuscitation Card

FULL CODE
In the event of a medical emergency,
I wish to have any and all means used to save my life.

Name: _____

Phone: _____

Emergency Contact: _____

Health Care Proxy _____

Phone: _____

This is my informed decision. My living will supports my decision.
It may be obtained from my family or health care proxy.

Understanding Your Living Will

**My Medical Living Will
Resuscitation Card**

FULL CODE EXCEPT CARDIAC ARREST

In the event of a medical emergency, I wish to receive aggressive treatment up until the point of cardiac arrest, at which time I wish to have nature take its course.

Name:_____

Phone: _____

Emergency Contact:_____

Health care Proxy_____

Phone: _____

This is my informed decision. My living will supports my decision.
It may be obtained from my family or health care proxy.

**My Medical Living Will
Resuscitation Card**

COMFORT CARE / HOSPICE CARE

I do not wish to receive any aggressive treatment measures.
If you have instituted these measures, you have my permission
to withdraw them completely. I wish to be kept free of pain
and anxiety and to have nature take its course.

Name:_____

Phone: _____

Emergency Contact:_____

Health care Proxy_____

Phone: _____

This is my informed decision. My living will supports my decision.
It may be obtained from my family or health care proxy.

84

Resources

U.S. Living Will Registry
P.O. Box 2789
Westfield, New Jersey 07091-2789
Phone: 1 800 LIV-WILL (1- 800-548-9455)
Fax: 1-908-654-1919
www.uslivingwillregistry.org

The U.S. Living Will Registry® electronically stores advance directives and makes them available to health care providers twenty-four hours a day via Internet, telephone, or facsimile. Founded in 1996, the U.S. Living Will Registry is a privately held organization that, for a fee, electronically stores advance directives, organ donor information, and emergency contact information, and makes them available to health care providers across the country through an automated system.

Aging with Dignity
P.O. Box 1661
Tallahassee, FL 32302-1661
Office: 820 East Park Avenue Suite D100
Tallahassee FL 32301-2600
Phone: (888) 594-7437
www.agingwithdignity.org

Founded in 1996, this organization provides practical information, advice, and legal tools to ensure that an individual's wishes and those of loved ones will be respected. The organization helps families plan and receive the care patients want in case of a serious illness. The organization provides information and resources to countless organizations at the local community level that are working to promote dignified care at the end of life.

To date, Aging with Dignity has worked with more than 5 million American families and more than 8,000 organizations.

Terri Schindler Schiavo Foundation (TSSF)
5562 Central Avenue, Suite 2
St. Petersburg, FL 33707
www.terrisfight.org

This nonprofit organization, incorporated in 2001 to fight for the life of Terri Schindler Schiavo (TSSF), focuses on educating the public about current guardianship laws and state laws regarding withdrawing life support measures. The TSSF also provides information and resources on advanced directives, medical futility policies, and individual constitutional rights. The TSSF recognizes the dangers associated with end of life decisions and provides the tools necessary for families to address these decisions with the committed belief that all human life is sacred.

Americans for the Better Care of the Dying
1700 Diagonal Road, Suite 635
Alexandria, VA 22314
Phone: (703) 647-8505
abcd-caring.org

Founded in 1997, this nonprofit organization's focus is ensuring that all Americans can count on good end-of-life care. It educates the public on improved pain management, better financial reimbursement systems, enhanced continuity of care, support for family care-givers, and changes in public policy. It offers an electronic newsletter, "ABCD Exchange." The site offers links to topics such as advance care planning, aging, care giving, chronic illness, end-of-life, hospice, pain management, palliative care, grief, bereavement and counseling, health care quality improvement, and public policy and law.

Death with Dignity National Center
520 Southwest 6th Avenue, Suite 1030
Portland, OR 97204
Phone: (503) 228-4415
www.deathwithdignity.org

The mission of this organization is to expand end-of-life choices and advance the legalization of physician aid in dying. Its Web site tracks end-of-life choice legislation at the state and federal levels and reports on international legislation news. Resources provided include a table of major religious groups' positions on assisted dying, results of national polling on end-of-life choices, suggested readings, a glossary, and information on Oregon's Death with Dignity Act.

American Bar Association
Chicago Headquarters
321 North Clark Street
Chicago, IL 60610
(312) 988-5000
www.abanet.org
Washington D.C. Office
740 15th Street, N.W.
Washington, DC 20005-1019
(202) 662-1000

The mission of the American Bar Association is to be the national representative of the legal profession, serving the public and the profession by promoting justice, professional excellence, and respect for the law. The Web site provides numerous resources for the consumer, including lawyer referrals and dozens of articles on legal topics such as advance directives, living wills, and health care power of attorney.

Legal Services Corporation
3333 K Street, NW
Washington, DC 20007
Phone: (202) 295-1500
www.lsc.gov

Created in 1974, this private, nonprofit corporation was established by Congress to ensure equal access to justice under the law for all Americans by providing civil legal assistance to those who otherwise would be unable to afford it. The corporation supports the free Legal Aid offices in all fifty states.

The National Senior Citizens Law Center (NSCLS)
1101 14th Street., NW Suite 400
Washington, DC 20005
Phone: (202) 289-6976
www.nsclc.org
Los Angeles, CA Office
3435 Wilshire Boulevard, Suite 2860
Los Angeles, CA 90010-1938
Phone: (213) 639-0930
Oakland, CA Office
1330 Broadway, Suite 525
Oakland, CA 94612
Phone: (510) 663-1055

This organization promotes the independence and well-being of low-income older individuals, as well as persons with disabilities. NSCLC advocates through litigation, legislative and agency representation, and assistance to attorneys and paralegals in field programs. The Web site includes federal rights materials, an online library, resources for advocates and consumers, related links, and a list of NSCLC publications.

National Academy of Elder Law Attorneys (NAELA)
1604 North Country Club Road
Tucson, Arizona 85716
Phone: (520) 881-4005
www.naela.com

The National Academy of Elder Law Attorneys, Inc. is a non-profit association comprised of attorneys in the private and public sectors who deal with legal issues affecting the elderly and disabled. Members also include judges, professors of law, and students. Some of the issues NAELA members assist their clients with are: public benefits, probate and estate planning, guardianship/conservatorship, and health and long-term care planning.

American Association of Retired Persons (AARP)
601 E Street, NW
Washington, DC 20049
Phone: 1-888-867-2277
www.aarp.org

This nonprofit organization serves people age fifty and older. The Legal Services Network provides members with access to more than 1,000 lawyers across the country who offer reduced fees for legal services. The Web site's "Internet Resources on Aging" link provides information on hundreds of topics, including links to sites that deal with end-of-life issues. The Legal Counsel for the Elderly division distributes several publications relating to living trusts and other end-of-life decisions.

Organ Donation
The U.S. Department of Health and Human Services
200 Independence Avenue, SW
Washington, D.C. 20201
Phone: (202) 619-0257
www.organdonor.gov

The official U.S. Government web site for organ and tissue donation and transplantation, this site is maintained by the Health Resources and Services Administration. The site lists organ procurement organizations for all fifty states. These organizations evaluate potential donors, discuss donation with family members, arrange for the surgical removal of donated organs; and preserve organs and arrange for their distribution according to national organ sharing policies.

Glossary

Advance directive: A legal written statement that is prepared in advance of an event. A living will is an example of an advance directive.

Advanced cardiac life-support protocols (ACLS): A set of techniques and medications designed to restore blood pressure and correct or restore the rhythm of your heart.

Angioplasty: A procedure to open a blockage in a blood vessel in the heart.

Arrhythmia: Abnormal beating of the heart.

Asystole: A cardiac standstill with no cardiac output, eventually occurring in all dying patients.

Attorney-in-fact: A person named in a written power of attorney to act on behalf of the person who signs the document.

Cardiac arrest: An abrupt temporary or permanent cessation of the heartbeat.

Cardiopulmonary resuscitation (CPR): The initial form of resuscitation that provides oxygen to the lungs to restore delivery of blood to the heart and brain.

Chemical code: The code that reflects the wishes of the patient to be treated with medications only. No other procedures are to be used.

Code status: A designation by health care workers that determines the type of care the patient is to receive.

Comfort Care: The code status that allows health care workers to make the patient comfortable and relieve pain, but not take any measures to save or extend the patient's life.

Defibrillation: A form of electrical therapy used when the heart is in an abnormal and lethal rhythm.

Defibrillator: An electronic device used to restore a regular heartbeat by applying an electric shock to it.

Do Not Intubate (DNI): An order that states that a patient does not wish to be placed on a ventilator.

Do Not Resuscitate (DNR): The designation intended for those who have expressed their wishes to be allowed to die naturally if they are found with no pulse or not breathing.

Durable power of attorney: A document that names an agent to make decisions regarding a person's property, finances, and assets if the person is unable to make them himself or herself.

Endotracheal intubation: See intubation.

Feeding tube: A surgically inserted tube that allows nutritional supplements to be delivered directly into the stomach.

Full Code Except Cardiac Arrest: The status code that is similar to Full Code except if the patient goes into cardiac arrest, health care workers will not try to revive the patient.

Full code: The code status in which the patient desires any and all resuscitative measures.

Health care power of attorney: A document that allows a person to designate who will have the authority to make health care decisions on their behalf if they are unconscious, mentally incompetent, or otherwise unable to make such decisions. Also referred to as a medical power of attorney.

Health care proxy: The person authorized to make decisions for a patient if the patient becomes unable to make those decisions.

Hemodialysis: A process in which a patient is connected to a dialysis machine, which acts like the kidneys to filter out body waste normally cleared in urine.

Hold harmless statement: A document that states that a person will not seek legal action against health care workers nor the health care facility for following their wishes.

Hospice Care: The care given to a patient with a terminal illness who chooses comfort measures and no aggressive life support. The patient usually remains in his home environment and is kept comfortable with pain medications.

Informed consent: An indication that you understand all the risks and benefits involved with your decisions as well as the effects your decisions will have on yourself and others.

Intravenous antibiotics: Antibiotics that are delivered into veins through an intravenous line.

Intravenous fluids: Fluids delivered into veins through an intravenous line to provide medications or keep a patient hydrated.

Intubation: The procedure in which a plastic tube is placed in the windpipe and connected to a breathing machine to assist the patient in breathing.

Invasive comfort procedures: Pain and anxiety relief that is delivered by the use of a central intravenous line or surgical procedure.

Invasive emergency procedures: The category of procedures that includes emergency surgery, insertion of chest tubes, intravenous delivery of lifesaving medications, and other lifesaving procedures.

Invasive procedures: A variety of treatments to provide lifesaving treatments.

Living will: A living will is a legal document in which patients are able to state in advance their desire to receive, or to withhold, life-support procedures when they are permanently unconscious or terminally ill and unable to make informed decisions.

Living will card: A card carried by the patient which summarizes their living will wishes

Long-term mechanical ventilation: Treatment in which a patient that is assisted in breathing by a machine until he or she is able to breathe on their own.

No code: The code designation that is basically the same as a DNR order.

Organ donor: A person who wishes to donate their organs.

Pacemaker: An electrical device for stimulating or steadying the heartbeat or reestablishing the rhythm of an arrested heart.

Parenteral nutrition: A form of nutrition that is delivered into a vein through an intravenous line, rather than through the digestive system.

Passive euthanasia: A death not inflicted with drugs and in which a person is allowed to die naturally.

Peritoneal dialysis: The procedure in which a dialysis solution is place into the abdomen. Blood flows through the solution, cleaning the blood, and then the solution is drained from the body.

Persistent vegetative state (PVS): A condition of patients with severe brain damage and coma in which the patient has progressed to a state of wakefulness without detectable awareness.

Resuscitation: A medical procedure that seeks to restore cardiac and/or respiratory function to individuals who have sustained a cardiac and/or respiratory arrest.

Slow Code: The status code used by health care workers to describe situations where it is easier to delay treatment rather than determine what level of treatment the patient wants.

Stabilization: The treatment medical workers provide to keep a patient's condition from worsening.

Surrogate decision maker: A person designated by the patient to make medical decisions if the patient is unable to make the decisions for himself or herself.

Terminal condition: Any health condition that does not respond to sound medical treatment.

Thrombolytics: Medications used to dissolve blood clots.

Tracheotomy: A surgical procedure in which a breathing tube is inserted into the windpipe.

Ventilator: A machine that assists the patient who cannot breathe on his or her own.

Bibliography

Bartholome WG. "Do not resuscitate" orders: accepting responsibility." *Arch Intern Med* 148 (1988):2345-46.

Beach MC, Morrison RS. "The effect of Do-Not-Resuscitate Orders on Physician Decision-Making." *JAGS* 2002;50:2057-61.

Bedell SE, Delbanco TL. "Choices about cardio-pulmonary resuscitation in the hospital. When do physicians talk with patients?" *N Engl J Med.* 1984; 310(17):1089-93.

Bedell SE, Pelle D, Maher Pl et al. Do-not-resuscitate orders for critically ill patients in the hospital. "How are they used and what is their impact?" *JAMA* 256 (1986):233-37.

Crippen D, Levy M, Truog R, Whetstine L, Luce J. "Debate: what constitutes 'terminality' and how does it relate to a living will?" *Crit Care* 4 (2000):333-8.

Culver CM "Advance directives." *Psychol Public Law Policy* 4(3) (1988):676-87.

Degenholz HB, Rhee Y, Arnold RM. "The relationship between living will and dying in place." *Ann Int Med* 141 (2004):113-17.

Eibach U. "Patient self-determination — reflections on critical and responsible management." *Pflege* 16(5) (2003):289-96. (Abstract in English).

Eisendrath SJ, Jonsen AR. "The living will. Help or hindrance?" *JAMA* 249(15):(1983):2054-8.

Emergency Cardiac Care Committee and Subcommittees, American Heart Association. Guidelines for cardiopulmonary resuscitation and Emergency Cardiac Care, VIII: ethical considerations in resuscitation. *JAMA* 268 (1992):2282-88.

Goodman MD, Tarnoff M, Slotman GJ. "Effect of Advanced Directives on the Management of Elderly Critically Ill Patients." *Critical Care Medicine* 26, No 4 (1998):701-04.

Henneman EA, Baird B, Bellany PE. "Effect of Do-Not-Resuscitate Orders On The Nursing Care of Critically Ill Patients." *Am Journal of Critical Care* (1994):Vol 3:6:467-72.

Hewitt WJ, Marco CA. "DNR: Does it Mean "Do Not Treat"." *ACEPNEWS*, June (2004): 3.

Hilden HM, Louhiala P, Palo J. "End of life decisions: attitudes of Finnish physicians." *J Med Ethics* 30(4) (2004): 362-5.

Keenan CH, Kish SK. "The influence of Do-Not-Resuscitate Orders on Care Provided for Patients in the Surgical Intensive Care Unit of a Cancer Center." *Critical Care Nursing Clinics of North America* Vol 12, No 3 Sep (2000) 385-90.

La Puma J, Silverstein MD, Stocking CE et al. "Life-sustaining treatment. A prospective study of patients with DNR orders in a teaching hospital." *Arch Intern Med* 148 (1988): 2193-98.

Landis JR, Koch GG. "The measurement of observer agreement for categorical data." *Biometrics* 33 (1977):159-74.

Larson DG, Tobin DR. "End-of-Life Conversations Evolving Practice and Theory." *JAMA* 284 (2000):1573-78.

Lewandowski W, Daly B, Mclish DK, Juknialis BW et al. "Treatment and care of "do not resuscitate" patients in a medical intensive care unit." *Heart Lung* (1985) 14:175-81.

Manthous CA. "Are living wills useful? In search of a new paradigm." *Conn Med* 67(5) (2003): 283-90.

McDonald DD, Deloge JA, Joslin N et al. "Communicating end-of-life preferences." *West J Nurs Res* 25(6) (2003): 667-75.

Miles SH, Crawford R, Shultz AL. "The do-not-resuscitate order in a teaching hospital." *Ann Intern Med.* 96 (1982):660-64.

Morrison MF. "Obstacles to doctor-patient communication at the end of life."

O'Toole EE, Younger SJ, Juknialis BW. "Evaluation of treatment limitation policy with specific treatment limiting order page." *Arch Intern Med,* 1994 Feb 28;154 (4):425-32.

Presidents Commission for the study of Ethical Problems in Medicine and Biomedical Research. *Deciding to forego life-sustaining treatment: ethical, medical and legal issues in treatment decisions.* Washington, DC: US Government Printing Office, 1983.

Rich BA. "Current legal status of advanced directives in the United States." Wien Klin Wochenschr 116(13) (2004): 420-26. (Abstract Only).

Schneider CE, Fagerlin A. "Enough, The Failure of the Living Will." *Hastings Center Report.* March–April 2004.

Shelly SI, Zahorchak RM, Gambril CDS. "Aggressiveness of Nursing Care for those with do not resuscitate orders." *Nurs Res.* (1987):36:157-62.

Sherman DA, Branum K. "Critical care nurses' perceptions of appropriate care of the patient with orders not to resuscitate." *Heart & Lung* Vol 24, No 4 p 321-29.

Standards for cardiopulmonary resuscitation (CPR) and emergency cardiac care (ECC): medico legal considerations and recommendations. *JAMA* 255 (1986):2979-84.

Steinberg MD, Youngner SJ, eds. *End-of-Life Decisions: A Psychosocial Pa.* C.S. Title 20; Ch 54; Advanced Directives for Health Care, Sections 5401-16.

Thibault-Prevost J, Jensen LA, Hodgins M. "Critical Nurses' perception of DNR Status." *Journal of Nursing scholarship.* Third quarter (2000): 259-65.

Tonelli M. "Pulling the Plug on Living Wills: A Critical Analysis of Advanced Directives." Chest 110(3): 816-22. September 1996.

Tulsky JA, Fisher GS, Rose MR et al. "Opening the black box: How do physicians communicate about advanced directives?" *Ann Intern Med.* 129(1998): 441-49.

U.S. Census Bureau, *2004 Population Estimates, Census 1990, Census 2000* <http://www.census.gov>.

Uhlmann, RF, Cassel CK, McDonald WJ. "Some treatment-withholding implications of no code orders in academic hospital." *Critical Care Medicine* 12 (1984): 879-81.

Van Norman GA. "Ethical Challenges in the Anesthetic Care of the Geriatric Patient." Syllabus on Geriatric

Anesthesiology, *American Society of Anesthesiologists.*

Younger SJ. "Do-not-resuscitate orders: no longer a secret but still a problem." *Hastings Cent Rep* 17 (1987): 24-33.

Index

A

activation of living will, 10, 37–48
advance directive for health care, 5, 16, 74
advanced cardiac life support protocols (ACLS), 50
alternate proxy, 13
American Association of Retired Persons (AARP), 65
amputation, 15
angina, 20
angioplasty, 58
anxiety, 46
asthma, 27
attorney, 32, 45, 62–64, 66
    fees, 64, 65
attorney-in-fact, 8
automated implanted cardiac defibrillator (AICD), 20

B

bleeding stroke, 42
blood, 58, 59
blood-borne diseases, 58
blood platelets, 58
blood products, 58, 59
blood transfusions, 15
blood work, 20, 43
boilerplate living will, 32, 62
brain dead, 45

I

implanted defibrillator, 60
implants, 69
incurable illness, 17
individualization of living will, 18, 32
informed consent, 18
  lack of, 32, 33
initial care, 40
*Initial Patient Safety Investigations and the Living
  Will,* 19
Internet, 32
intravenous antibiotics, 55
intravenous fluids, 54
invasive comfort procedures, 54
invasive emergency procedures, 53, 54
invasive procedures, 27, 53

J

joint replacement, 69

K

kidney failure, 59, 60

L

laboratory work, 20
last will and testament, 5, 16, 37, 73
legal guardian, 11
Legal Services Network, 65
living will
  activation, 10, 37–48, 75
  basics, 3–16
  challenging, 46, 47
  changes, 75
  code status, 21–31
  code status not to include, 26–28

M

U

Uniform Rights of the Terminally Ill Act, 9
updating living will, 47, 48
U.S. Living Will Registry, 4, 71

V

ventilation
    see ventilator
ventilator, 6, 27, 50
volunteer attorney, 65

W

white blood cells, 58
witnesses, 66, 67

About the Author

Dr. Ferdinando L. Mirarchi is chairman of the Department of Emergency Medicine of Hamot Medical Center in Erie, Pennsylvania. He is an assistant clinical professor of the Department of Emergency Medicine, West Penn Allegheny Health System, Allegheny General Hospital, Drexel University School of Medicine. He is also a fellow of the American Academy of Emergency Medicine and the American College of Emergency Physicians.

After completing his undergraduate studies at Temple University in Philadelphia, Dr. Mirarchi graduated from the medical school at Western University of Health Sciences College of Osteopathic Medicine in Pomona, California.

Dr. Mirarchi has been nationally and internationally published in the field of emergency medicine. He has also been interviewed on the subject of living wills by both local and national media, including *USA Today*, the Associated Press, and ABC News. Dr. Mirarchi serves on the consulting staff for www.emedicine.com.

Dr. Mirarchi may be reached by email at: drfred@paer.org.

Consumer Health Titles from Addicus Books
Visit our online catalog at www.AddicusBooks.com

Organizations, associations, corporations, hospitals, and other groups may qualify for special discounts when ordering more than twenty-four copies. For more information, please contact the Special Sales Department at Addicus Books. Phone (402) 330-7493. Email: info@AddicusBooks.com